BOB DYLAN

Learning to play a musical instrument is one of the most satisfying experiences a person can have. Being able to play along with other musicians makes that even more rewarding. This collection of Bob Dylan songs is designed to make it easy to enjoy the fun of gathering with friends and family to make music together.

The music for each song displays the chord diagrams for five instruments: ukulele, baritone ukulele, guitar, mandolin and banjo. The chord diagrams indicate basic, commonly used finger positions. More advanced players can substitute alternate chord formations.

Arranged by Mark Phillips

ISBN 978-1-70513-428-3

HAL•LEONARD®

Visit Hal Leonard Online at
www.halleonard.com

World headquarters, contact:
Hal Leonard
7777 West Bluemound Road
Milwaukee, WI 53213
Email: info@halleonard.com

In Europe, contact:
Hal Leonard Europe Limited
1 Red Place
London, W1K 6PL
Email: info@halleonardeurope.com

In Australia, contact:
Hal Leonard Australia Pty. Ltd.
4 Lentara Court
Cheltenham, Victoria, 3192 Australia
Email: info@halleonard.com.au

Tuning

Standard Ukulele
(Soprano, Concert, Tenor)

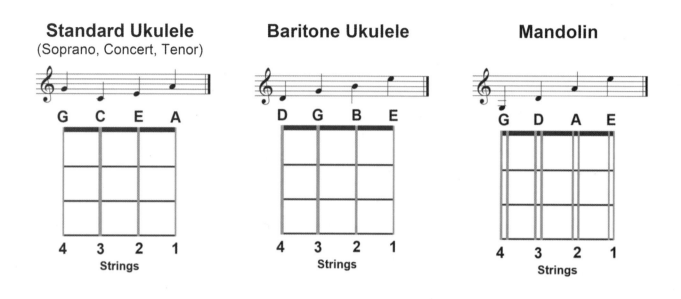

Baritone Ukulele

Mandolin

Banjo
(Open G Tuning)

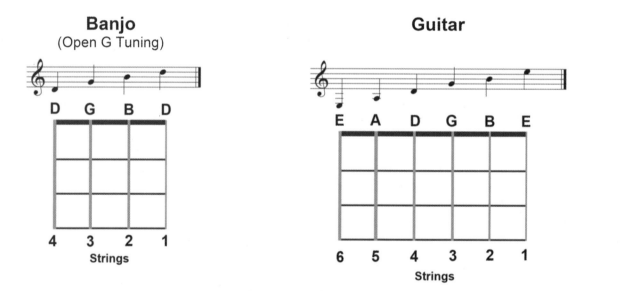

Guitar

All banjo chord formations illustrated in this book are based on "Open G" tuning. If an alternate tuning is used the banjo player can read the chord letters for the songs and disregard the diagrams.

Standard Ukulele

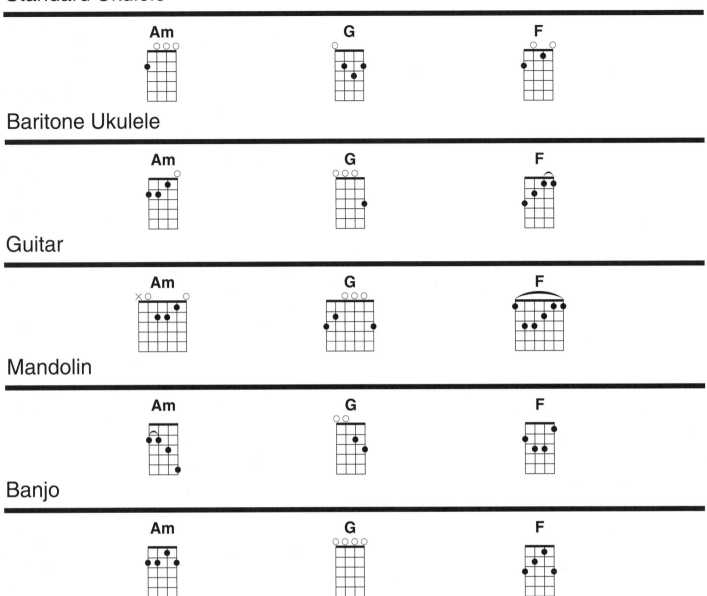

Baritone Ukulele

Guitar

Mandolin

Banjo

All Along the Watchtower
Words and Music by Bob Dylan

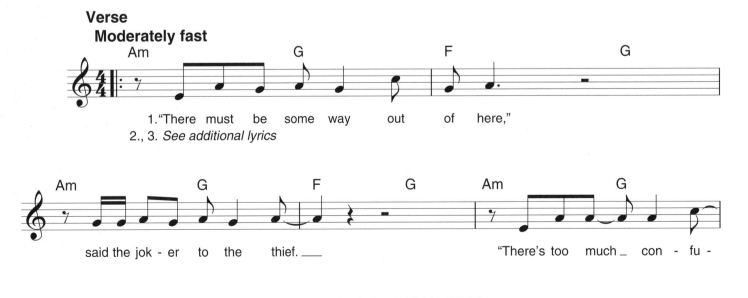

Verse
Moderately fast

1."There must be some way out of here,"
2., 3. *See additional lyrics*

said the jok-er to the thief. ___ "There's too much_ con-fu-

- sion, I can't get ___ no re - lief. ___

Bus' - ness - men, ___ they drink my wine, ___ plow - men ___ dig my earth. ___

___ None of them a - long ___ the line ___

know what an - y of it is worth." ___

Play 3 times

Additional Lyrics

2. "No reason to get excited," the thief, he kindly spoke.
   "There are many here among us who feel that life is but a joke.
   But you and I, we've been through that, and this not our fate.
   So let us not talk falsely now, the hour's getting late."

3. All along the watchtower, princes kept the view,
   While all the women came and went, barefoot servants, too.
   Outside in the distance a wildcat did growl.
   Two riders were approaching, the wind began to howl.

Standard Ukulele

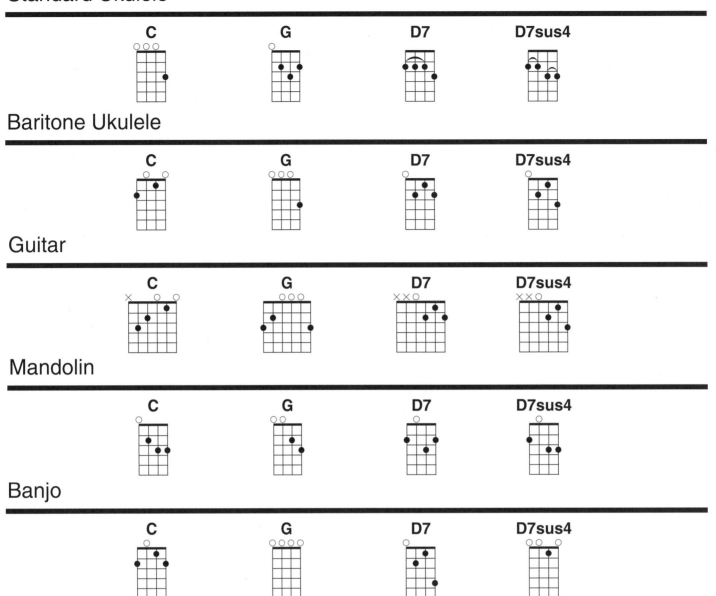

Baritone Ukulele

Guitar

Mandolin

Banjo

All I Really Want to Do

Words and Music by Bob Dylan

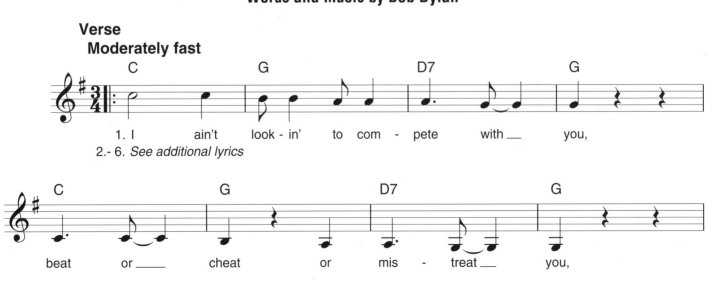

Verse
Moderately fast

1. I ain't look - in' to com - pete with ___ you,
2.- 6. *See additional lyrics*

beat or ___ cheat or mis - treat ___ you,

Chorus

Lyrics under music:
sim - pli - fy you, ___ clas - si - fy ___ you, de - ny, ___ ___ de - fy ___ or cru - ci - fy ___ you.

All I ___ real - ly ___ want to do ___ ___ is, ba - by, be ___ friends with ___ you.

1.- 5. | 6.

2. No, and

Additional Lyrics

2. No, and I ain't lookin' to fight with you,
Frighten you or uptighten you,
Drag you down or drain you down,
Chain you down or bring you down.

3. I ain't lookin' to block you up,
Shock or knock or lock you up,
Analyze you, categorize you,
Finalize you or advertise you.

4. I don't want to straight-face you,
Race or chase you, track or trace you,
Or disgrace you or displace you,
Or define you or confine you.

5. I don't want to meet your kin,
Make you spin or do you in,
Or select you or dissect you,
Or inspect you or reject you.

6. I don't want to fake you out,
Take or shake or forsake you out.
I ain't lookin' for you to feel like me,
See like me or be like me.

Standard Ukulele

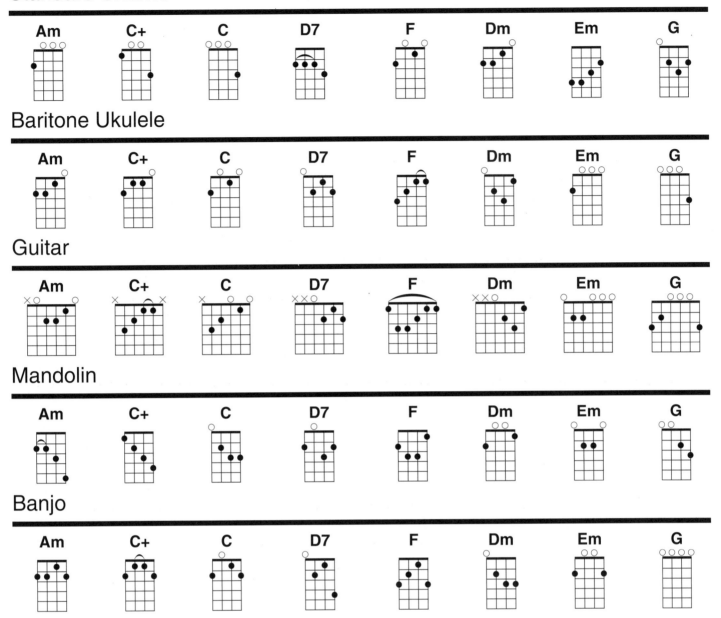

| Am | C+ | C | D7 | F | Dm | Em | G |

Baritone Ukulele

| Am | C+ | C | D7 | F | Dm | Em | G |

Guitar

| Am | C+ | C | D7 | F | Dm | Em | G |

Mandolin

| Am | C+ | C | D7 | F | Dm | Em | G |

Banjo

| Am | C+ | C | D7 | F | Dm | Em | G |

Ballad of a Thin Man
Words and Music by Bob Dylan

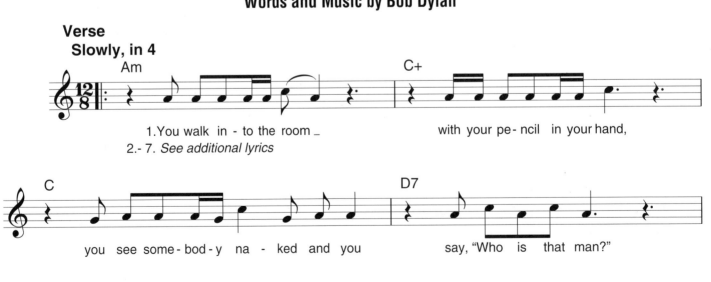

Verse
Slowly, in 4

1. You walk in - to the room _ with your pe - ncil in your hand,
2. - 7. *See additional lyrics*

you see some - bod - y na - ked and you say, "Who is that man?"

Additional Lyrics

2. You raise up your head
   And you ask, "Is this where it is?"
   And somebody points to you and says,
   "It's his."
   And you say, "What's mine?"
   And somebody else says, "Well,
   What is?"
   And you say, "Oh my God
   Am I here all alone?"

3. You hand in your ticket
   And you go watch the geek,
   Who immediately walks up to you
   When he hears you speak,
   And says, "How does it feel
   To be such a freak?"
   And you say, "Impossible"
   As he hands you a bone.

4. You've been with the professors
   And they've all liked your looks.
   With great lawyers you have
   Discussed lepers and crooks.
   You've been through all of
   F. Scott Fitzgerald's books.
   You're very well read,
   It's well known.

5. Well, the sword swallower, he
   Comes up to you,
   And then he kneels,
   `He crosses himself,
   And then he clicks his high heels,
   And without further notice,
   He asks you how it feels,
   And he says, "Here is your throat back.
   Thanks for the loan."

6. Now you see this one-eyed midget
   Shouting the word "now,"
   And you say, "For what reason?"
   And he says, "How?"
   And you say, "What does this mean?"
   And he screams back, "You're a cow.
   Give me some milk
   Or else go home."

7. Well, you walk into the room
   Like a camel and then you frown.
   You put your eyes in your pocket
   And your nose on the ground.
   There ought to be a law
   Against you comin' around.
   You should be made
   To wear earphones.

Standard Ukulele

Baritone Ukulele

Guitar

Mandolin

Banjo

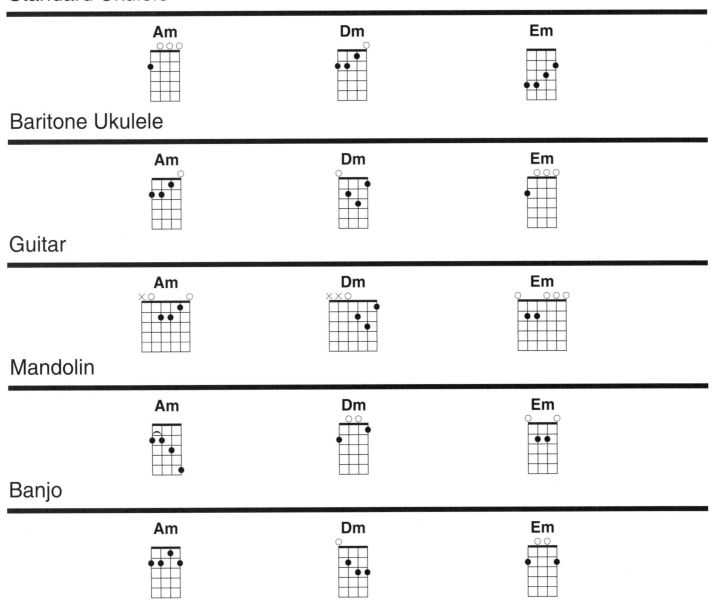

Beyond Here Lies Nothing

Words and Music by Bob Dylan and Robert C. Hunter

Moderately

Verse

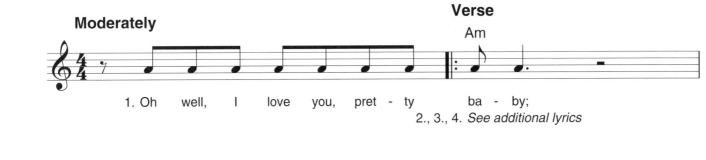

1. Oh well, I love you, pret - ty ba - by;

2., 3., 4. *See additional lyrics*

you're the on - ly love I've ev - er known. ___ Just as long as you stay

with me, the whole world is my throne.

Be-yond here lies noth-in', noth-in' we can call our

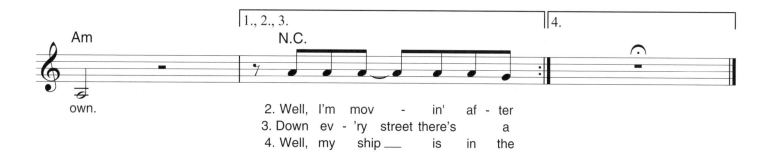

own.
2. Well, I'm mov - in' af - ter
3. Down ev - 'ry street there's a
4. Well, my ship is in the

Additional Lyrics

2. Well, I'm movin' after midnight
   Down boulevards of broken cars.
   Don't know what I'd do without it,
   Without this love that we call ours.
   Beyond here lies nothin',
   Nothin' but the moon and stars.

3. Down ev'ry street there's a window,
   And ev'ry window made of glass.
   We'll keep on lovin', pretty baby,
   For as long as love will last.
   Beyond here lies nothin'
   But the mountains of the past.

4. Well, my ship is in the harbor
   And the sails are spread.
   Listen to me, pretty baby;
   Lay your hand upon my head.
   Beyond here lies nothin',
   Nothin' done and nothin' said.

Standard Ukulele

Baritone Ukulele

Guitar

Mandolin

Banjo

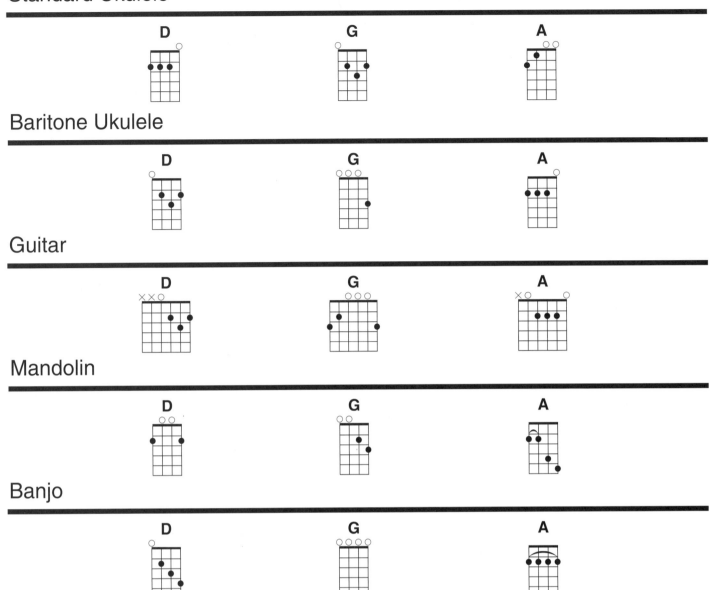

Blowin' in the Wind
Words and Music by Bob Dylan

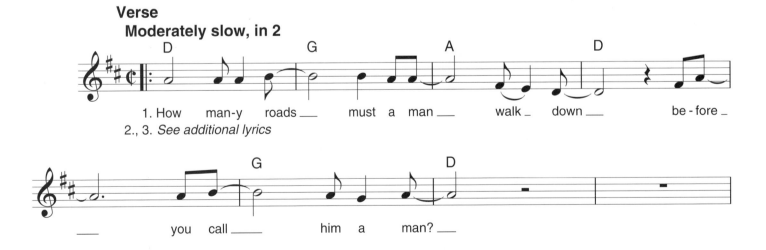

Verse
Moderately slow, in 2

1. How man-y roads ___ must a man ___ walk ___ down ___ be - fore
2., 3. *See additional lyrics*

___ you call ___ him a man? ___

How man-y seas ___ must the white ___ dove _ sail ___ be - fore _

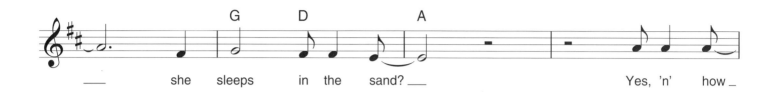

___ she sleeps in the sand? ___ Yes, 'n' how _

___ man-y times ___ must the can-non - balls _ fly ___ be - fore _

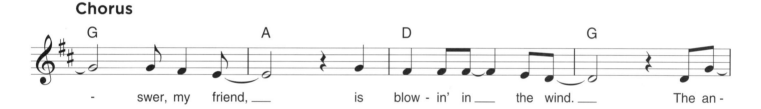

___ they're for - ev - er banned? ___ The an -

Chorus

- swer, my friend, ___ is blow - in' in ___ the wind. ___ The an -

- swer is blow-in' in the wind. ___   2., 3. Yes, 'n'

Additional Lyrics

2. Yes, 'n' how many years can a mountain exist
   Before it's washed to the sea?
   Yes, 'n' how many years can some people exist
   Before they're allowed to be free?
   Yes, 'n' how many times can a man turn his head
   Pretending he just doesn't see?

3. Yes, 'n' how many times must a man look up
   Before he can see the sky?
   Yes, 'n' how many ears must one man have
   Before he can hear people cry?
   Yes, 'n' how many deaths will it take till he knows
   That too many people have died?

Standard Ukulele

Baritone Ukulele

Guitar

Mandolin

Banjo

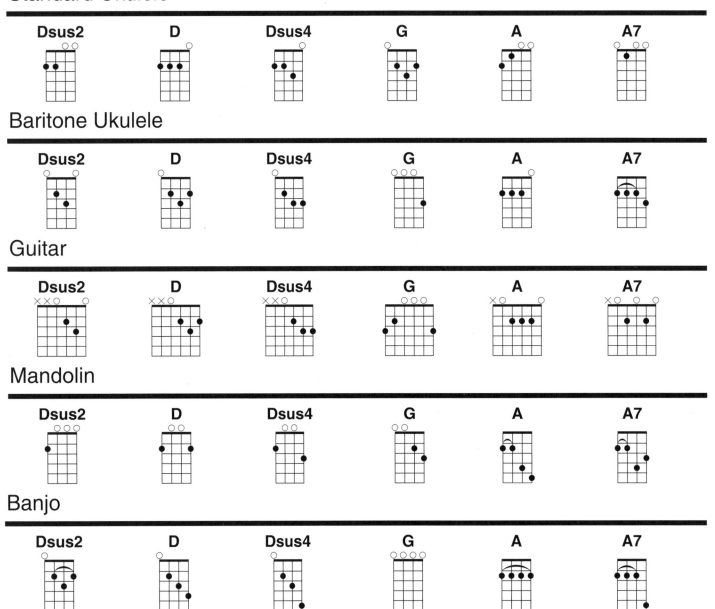

Buckets of Rain
Words and Music by Bob Dylan

Verse
Moderately, in 2

1. Buck - ets of rain, ___ buck - ets of tears. ___
2. - 5. *See additional lyrics*

Got all them buck - ets com - in' out of my ears. ___

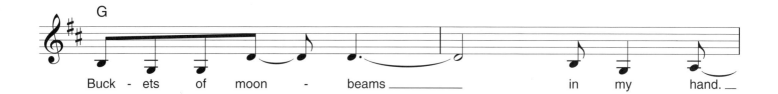

Buck - ets of moon - beams _____ in my hand. __

_____ You got all the love,

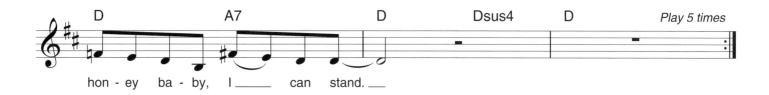

hon - ey ba - by, I _____ can stand. __

Play 5 times

Additional Lyrics

2. I been meek, and hard like an oak.
   I seen pretty people disappear like smoke.
   Friends will arrive, friends will disappear.
   If you want me, honey baby, I'll be here.

3. I like your smile and your fingertips,
   I like the way that you move your hips.
   I like the cool way you look at me.
   Everything about you is bringing me misery.

4. Little red wagon, little red bike.
   I ain't no monkey but I know what I like.
   I like the way you love me strong and slow.
   I'm takin' you with me, honey baby, when I go.

5. Life is sad, life is a bust.
   All ya can do is do what you must.
   You do what you must do and ya do it well.
   I do it for you, honey baby. Can't you tell?

Standard Ukulele

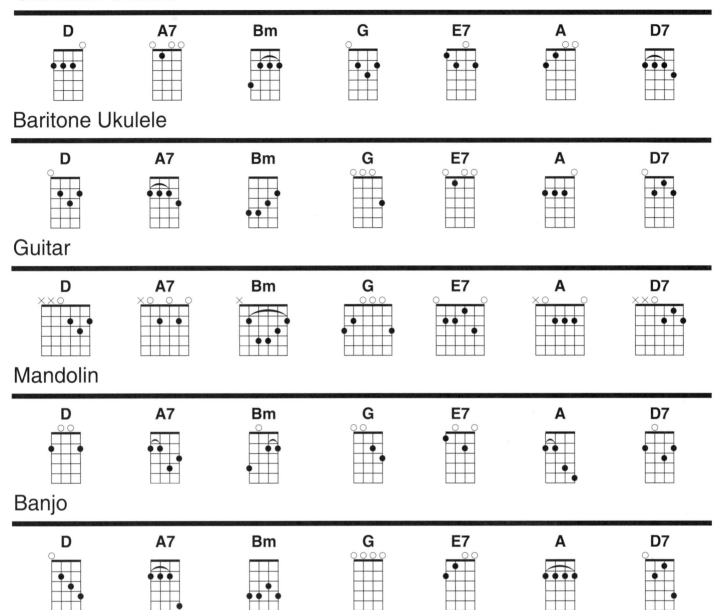

Baritone Ukulele

Guitar

Mandolin

Banjo

Don't Think Twice, It's All Right
Words and Music by Bob Dylan

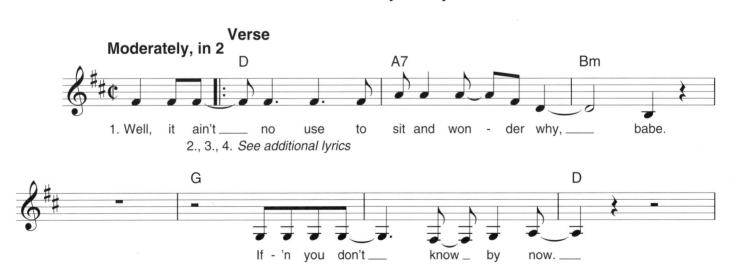

1. Well, it ain't ____ no use to sit and won - der why, ____ babe.
2., 3., 4. *See additional lyrics*

If - 'n you don't ____ know ____ by now. ____

An' it ain't no use to sit and won - der why, ___ babe.

It - 'll nev-er do some - how. When your roost -

- er ___ crows at the break ___ of dawn, ___ look out ___ your

win - dow and _____ I'll be gone. You're the ___

rea-son I'm ___ a - trav - el - in' ___ on. But don't ___ think ___ twice,

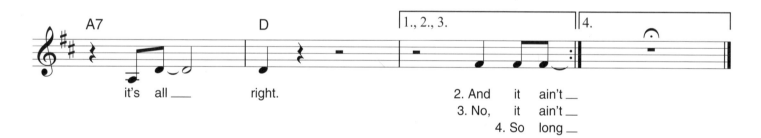

it's all ___ right.

2. And it ain't ___
3. No, it ain't ___
4. So long ___

Additional Lyrics

2. And it ain't no use in a-turnin' on your light, babe,
The light I never knowed.
An' it ain't no use in turnin' on your light, babe.
I'm on the dark side of the road.
But I wish there was somethin' you would do or say
To try and make me change my mind and stay.
We never did too much talkin' anyway.
But don't think twice, it's all right.

3. No, it ain't no use in callin' out my name, gal,
Like you never done before.
And it ain't no use in callin' out my name, gal;
I can't hear you anymore.
I'm a-thinkin' and a-wond'rin', walk-in' down the road,
I once loved a woman, a child I'm told.
I give her my heart but she wanted my soul.
But don't think twice, it's all right.

4. So long, honey babe;
Where I'm bound, I can't tell.
But goodbye's too good a word, babe,
So I'll just say fare thee well.
I ain't sayin' you treated me unkind;
You coulda done better but I don't mind.
You just kinda wasted my precious time.
But don't think twice, it's all right.

Standard Ukulele

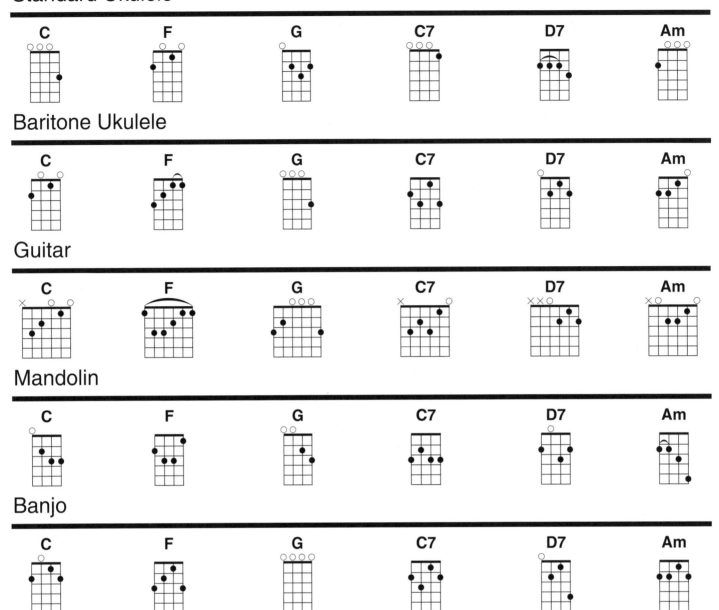

Baritone Ukulele

Guitar

Mandolin

Banjo

Duquesne Whistle
Words and Music by Bob Dylan and Robert C. Hunter

Verse
Moderately, in 2

1. Lis-ten to ___ that Du - quesne whi - stle blow - in',
2.- 5. *See additional lyrics*

Blow in' like ___ it's gon-na sweep my world ___ a- way. ___ I'm gon-na

D.C. al Fine

Interlude

Additional Lyrics

2. Listen to that Duquesne whistle blowin',
   Blowin' like she never blowed before.
   Blue light blinkin', red light glowin',
   Blowin' like she's at my chamber door.
   You smiling through the fence at me
   Just like you've always smiled before.
   Listen to that Duquesne whistle blowin',
   Blowin' like she ain't gonna blow no more.

3. Can't you hear that Duquesne whistle blowin',
   Blowin' like the sky's gonna blow apart?
   You're the only thing alive that keeps me goin'.
   You're like a time bomb in my heart.
   I can hear a sweet voice gently calling,
   Must be the Mother of our Lord.
   Listen to that Duquesne whistle blowin',
   Blowin' like my woman's on board.

4. Listen to that Duquesne whistle blowin',
   Blowin' like it's gonna blow my blues away.
   You ole rascal, I know exactly where you're goin'.
   I'll lead you there myself at the break of day.
   I wake up every morning with that woman in my bed.
   Everybody telling me she's gone to my head.
   Listen to that Duquesne whistle blowin',
   Blowin' like it's gonna kill me dead.

5. Can't you hear that Duquesne whistle blowin',
   Blowin' through another no-good town?
   The lights of my native land are glowin'.
   I wonder if they'll know me next time around.
   I wonder if that old oak tree's still standing,
   That old oak tree, the one we used to climb.
   Listen to that Duquesne whistle blowin',
   Blowin' like she's blowin' right on time.

Standard Ukulele

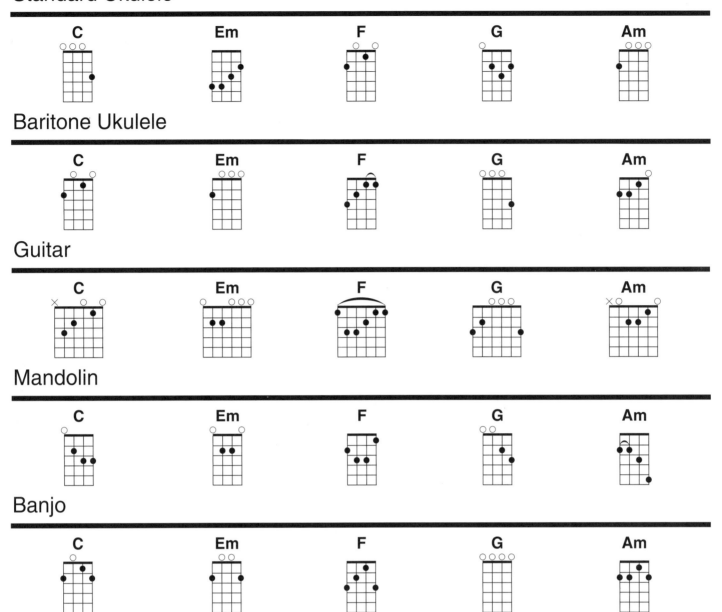

Baritone Ukulele

Guitar

Mandolin

Banjo

Forever Young
Words and Music by Bob Dylan

1. May God bless and keep you al-ways. May your wish-es all come true. May you
2., 3. *See additional lyrics*

al-ways do ___ for oth-ers ___ and let oth - ers do ___ for you.

Additional Lyrics

2. May you grow up to be righteous.
   May you grow up to be true.
   May you always know the truth
   And see the lights surrounding you.
   May you always be courageous,
   Stand upright and be strong,
   And may you stay forever young.

3. May your hands always be busy.
   May your feet always be swift.
   May you have a strong foundation
   When the winds of changes shift.
   May your heart always be joyful.
   May your song always be sung,
   And may you stay forever young.

Standard Ukulele

Baritone Ukulele

Guitar

Mandolin

Banjo

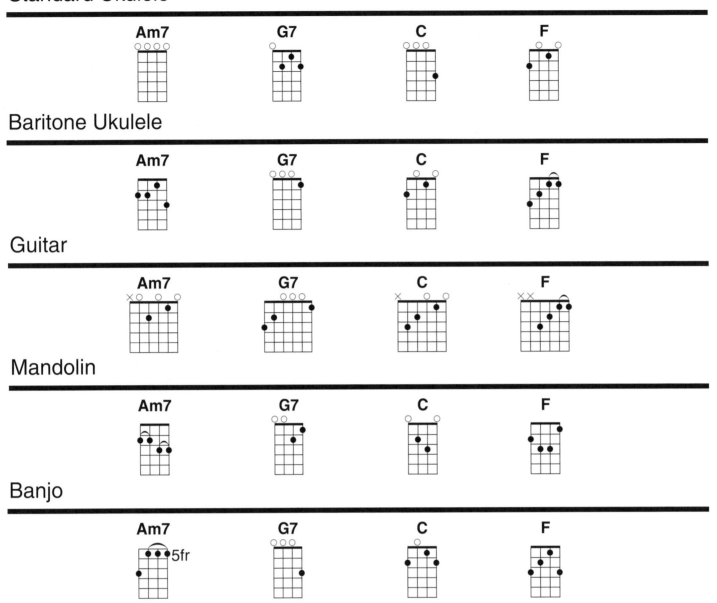

Girl from the North Country
Words and Music by Bob Dylan

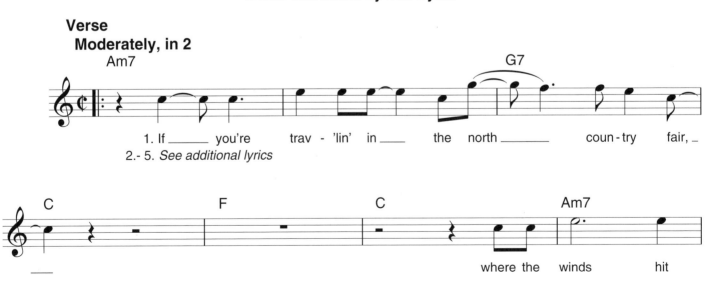

Verse
Moderately, in 2

1. If _____ you're trav - 'lin' in _____ the north _____ coun - try fair, _
2.- 5. *See additional lyrics*

where the winds hit

heav - y on the bor - der - line,

re - mem - ber me ___ to one ___ who lives there, ___

___ 'cause she _____ once was ___ a

Play 5 times

true love ___ of mine. ___

Additional Lyrics

2. If you go when the snowflakes storm,
   When the rivers freeze and summer ends,
   Please see she has a coat so warm
   To keep her from the howlin' winds.

3. Please see if her hair hangs long,
   If it rolls and flows all down her breast.
   Please see for me if her hair's hanging long,
   For that's the way I remember her best.

4. I'm wonderin' if she remembers me at all.
   Many times I've often prayed
   In the darkness of my night,
   In the brightness of my day.

5. So if you're travelin' in the north country fair,
   Where the winds hit heavy on the borderline,
   Remember me to one who lives there,
   'Cause she once was a true love of mine.

Standard Ukulele

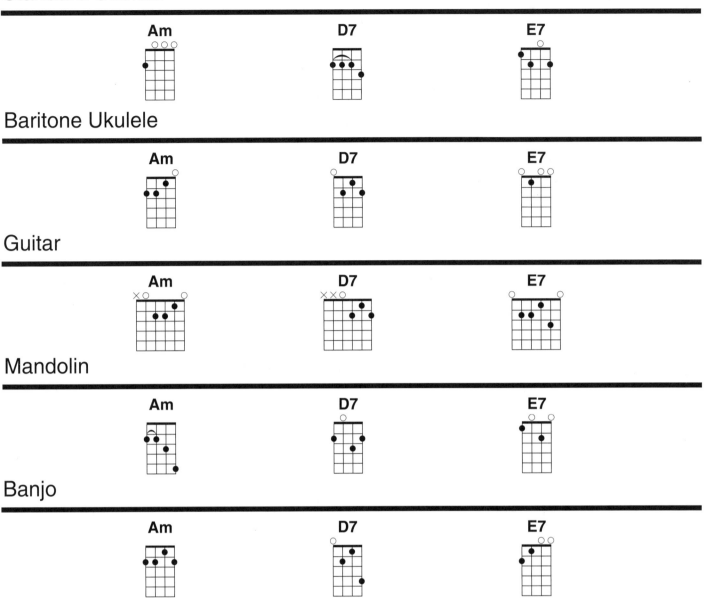

Baritone Ukulele

Guitar

Mandolin

Banjo

Gotta Serve Somebody
Words and Music by Bob Dylan

Verse
Moderately slow

1. You may be an am - bas - sa - dor ___ to Eng - land or France. ___
2., 3. *See additional lyrics*

You may like to gam - ble, you might like to dance. ___

You may __ be the heav - y - weight cham - pion of the world. __

You may be a so - cial - ite __ with a long ____ string of pearls. But you're gon - na have to

Chorus

D7

serve some - bod - y, yes in - deed, __ you're gon - na have to serve __

Am

__ some - bod - y.

E7

Well, it may be the dev - il or ____ it __

D7 ⌐—3—⌐ Am

____ may be the Lord, __ but you're gon - na have to serve some - bod - y.

1.- 6. 7.

2.- 7. You

Additional Lyrics

2. You might be a rock 'n' roll addict prancing on the stage.
   You might have drugs at your command, women in a cage.
   You may be a businessman or some high-degree thief.
   They may call you Doctor or they may call you Chief.

3. You may be a state trooper, you might be a young Turk.
   You may be the head of some big TV network.
   You may be rich or poor, you may be blind or lame.
   You may be living in another country under another name.

4. You may be a construction worker working on a home.
   You might be living in a mansion or you might live in a dome.
   You may own guns and you may even own tanks.
   You may be somebody's landlord, you may even own banks.

5. You may be a preacher with your spiritual pride.
   You may be a city councilman taking bribes on the side.
   You may be workin' in a barbershop, you may know how to cut hair.
   You may be somebody's mistress, may be somebody's heir.

6. You might like to wear cotton, might like to wear silk.
   You might like to drink whiskey, might like to drink milk.
   You might like to eat caviar, you might like to eat bread.
   You may be sleeping on the floor, sleeping in a king-sized bed.

7. You may call me Terry, you may call me Timmy.
   You may call me Bobby, you may call me Zimmy.
   You may call me R.J., you may call me Ray.
   You may call me anything, but no matter what you say…

Standard Ukulele

Baritone Ukulele

Guitar

Mandolin

Banjo

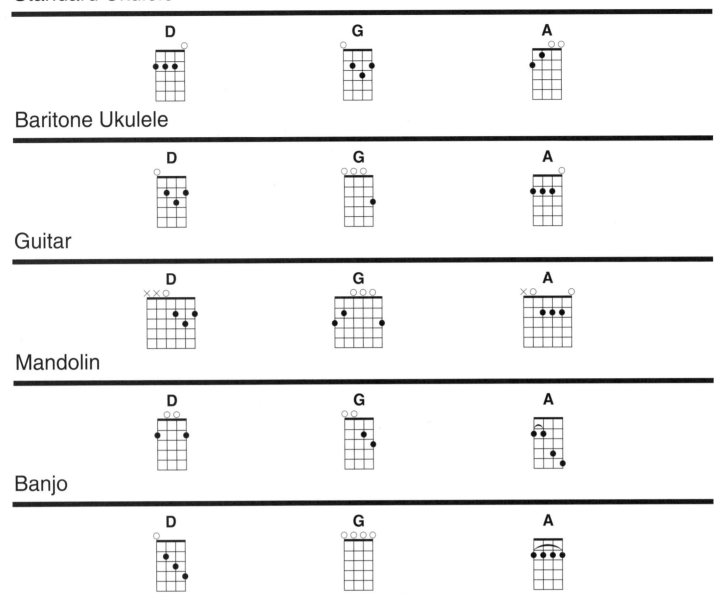

A Hard Rain's A-Gonna Fall
Words and Music by Bob Dylan

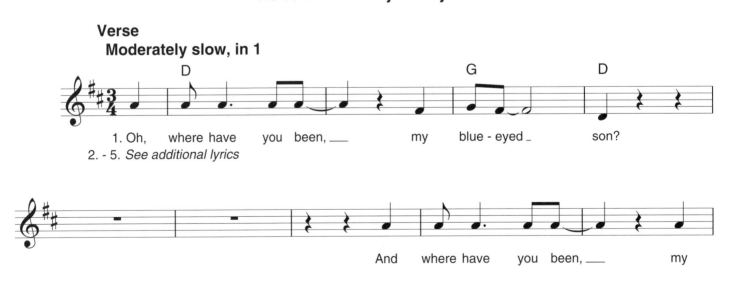

Verse
Moderately slow, in 1

1. Oh, where have you been, ___ my blue-eyed ___ son?
2. - 5. *See additional lyrics*

And where have you been, ___ my

Additional Lyrics

2. Oh, what did you see, my blue-eyed son?
   And what did you see, my darling young one?
   I saw a newborn baby with wild wolves all around it.
   I saw a highway of diamonds with nobody on it.
   I saw a black branch with blood that kept drippin'.
   I saw a room full of men with their hammers a-bleedin'.
   I saw a white ladder all covered with water.
   I saw ten thousand talkers whose tongues were all broken.
   I saw guns and sharp swords in the hands of young children.

3. And what did you hear, my blue-eyed son?
   And what did you hear, my darling young one?
   I heard the sound of a thunder that roared out a warnin'.
   I heard the roar of a wave that could drown the whole world.
   I heard one hundred drummers whose hands were a-blazin'.
   I heard ten thousand whisperin' and nobody listenin'.
   I heard one person starve; I heard many people laughin'.
   I heard the song of a poet who died in the gutter.
   I heard the sound of a clown who cried in the alley.

4. Oh, what did you meet, my blue-eyed son?
   And who did you meet, my darling young one?
   I met a young child beside a dead pony.
   I met a white man who walked a black dog.
   I met a young woman whose body was burning.
   I met a young girl; she gave me a rainbow.
   I met one man who was wounded in love.
   I met another man who was wounded in hatred.

5. And what'll you do now, my blue-eyed son?
   And what'll you do now, my darling young one?
   I'm a-goin' back out 'fore the rain starts a-fallin'.
   I'll walk to the depths of the deepest dark forest.
   Where the people are many and their hands are all empty.
   Where the pellets of poison are flooding their waters.
   Where the home in the valley meets the damp dirty prison.
   And the executioner's face is always well hidden.
   Where hunger is ugly, where the souls are forgotten.
   Where black is the color, where none is the number.
   And I'll tell it and speak it and think it and breathe it.
   And reflect from the mountain so all souls can see it.
   Then I'll stand on the ocean until I start sinkin'.
   But I'll know my song well before I start singin'.

Standard Ukulele

Baritone Ukulele

Guitar

Mandolin

Banjo

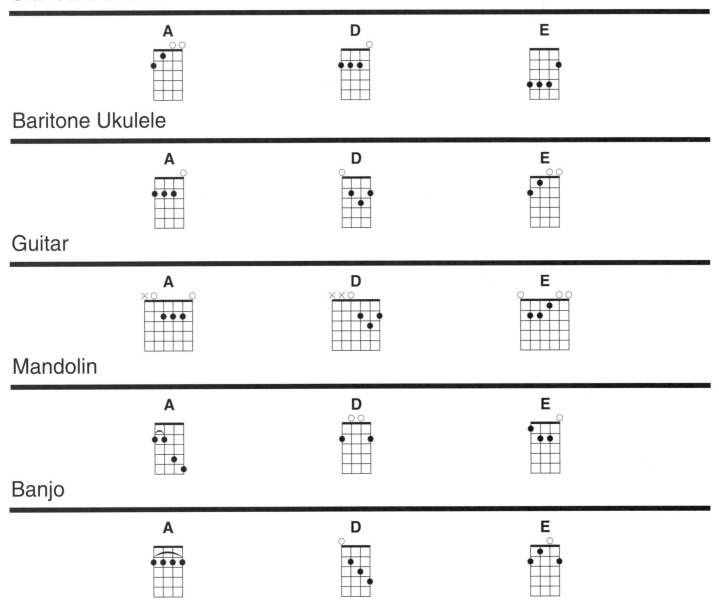

Highway 61 Revisited
Words and Music by Bob Dylan

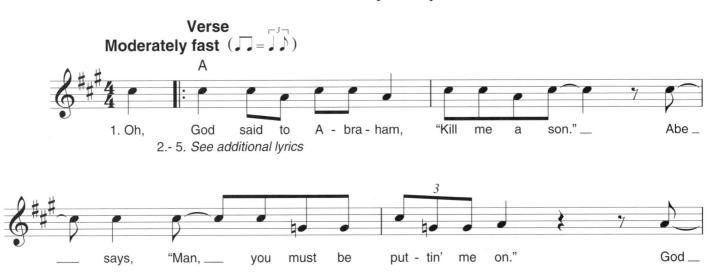

Verse
Moderately fast

A

1. Oh, God said to A - bra - ham, "Kill me a son." __ Abe __

2.- 5. *See additional lyrics*

__ says, "Man, __ you must be put - tin' me on." God __

_____ say, "No." _____ Abe _____ say, "What?" _____ God _____

_____ say, _____ "You can do what you want, _____ Abe, but _____ the

next time you see me com - in', you bet - ter run."

Well, Abe _____ says, "Where do you want this

kill - in' done?" _____ God _____ says, "Out on _____ High - way _____ Six - ty - one."

1.- 4.   5.

2., 3. Well,
4., 5. Now,

Additional Lyrics

2. Well, Georgia Sam, he had a bloody nose;
   Welfare Department, they wouldn't give him no clothes.
   He asked poor Howard, "Where can I go,"
   Howard said, "There's only one place I know."
   Sam said, "Tell me quick, man; I got to run."
   Ol' Howard just pointed with his gun
   And said, "That way down on Highway 61."

3. Well, Mack the Finger said to Louie the King,
   "I got forty red, white and blue shoe strings,
   And a thousand telephones that don't ring.
   Do you know where I can get rid of these things."
   And Louie the King said,
   "Let me think for a minute, son,"
   And he said, "Yes, I think it can be easily done.
   Just take everything down to Highway 61."

4. Now, the fifth daughter on the twelfth night
   Told the first father that things weren't right.
   "My complexion," she said, "is much too white."
   He said, "Come here and step into the light."
   He says, "Hmm, you're right.
   Let me tell the second mother this has been done."
   But the second mother was with the seventh son,
   And they were both out on Highway 61.

5. Now, the rovin' gambler, he was very bored.
   He was tryin' to create a next world war.
   He found a promoter who nearly fell off the floor.
   He said, "I never engaged in this kind of thing before,
   But yes, I think it can be very easily done.
   We'll just put some bleachers out in the sun
   And have it on Highway 61."

Standard Ukulele

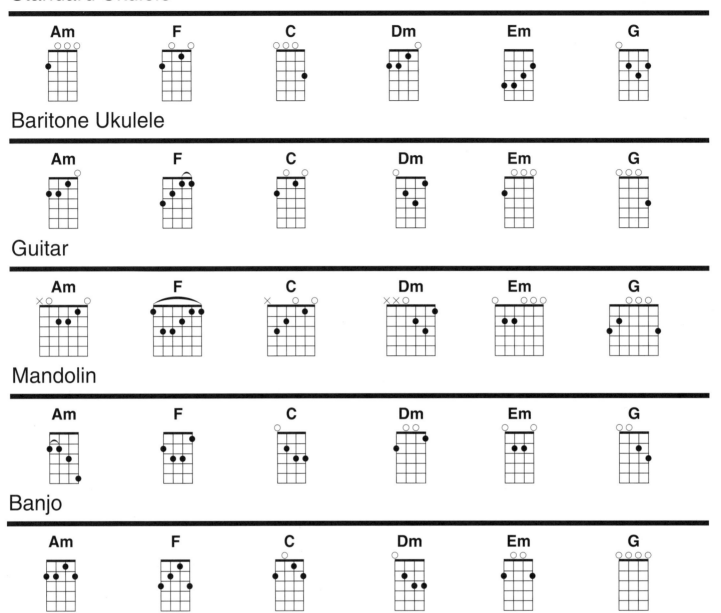

Baritone Ukulele

Guitar

Mandolin

Banjo

Hurricane
Words and Music by Bob Dylan and Jacques Levy

Verse
Moderately fast

1. Pis-tol shots ring out in a bar - room night. _
2.–11. *See additional lyrics*

En-ter Pat-ty Val - en-tine from the up - per hall. _

She sees a bar - tend - er in a pool of blood. _

Additional Lyrics

2. Three bodies lying there does Patty see,
   And another man named Bello movin' around mysteriously.
   "I didn't do it," he says, and he throws up his hands.
   "I was only robbing the register. I hope you understand.
   I saw 'em leavin'," he says, and he stops.
   "One of us had better call up the cops."
   And so Patty calls the cops,
   And they arrive on the scene with their red lights flashin'
   In the hot New Jersey night.

3. Meanwhile, far away in another part of town,
   Rubin Carter and a couple of friends are drivin' around.
   The number one contender for the middleweight crown
   Had no idea what kinda shit was about to go down
   When the cop pulled him over to the side of the road.
   Just like the time before and the time before that,
   In Patterson that's just the way things go.
   If you're black, you might as well not show up on the street
   'Less you wanna draw the heat.

4. Alfred Bello had a partner and he had a rap for the cops.
   Him and Arthur Dexter Bradley were just out prowlin' around.
   He said, "I saw two men runnin' out; they looked
   Like middleweights.
   They jumped into a white car with out-of-state plates."
   And Miss Patty Valentine just nodded her head.
   Cop said, "Wait a minute, boys. This one's not dead."
   So they took him to the infirmary,
   And though this man could hardly see,
   They told him he could identify the guilty men.

5. Four in the morning and they haul Rubin in.
   They took him to the hospital and they brought him upstairs.
   The wounded man looks up through his one dyin' eye,
   Say, "Why'd you bring him in here for? He ain't the guy!"
   Here's the story of the Hurricane,
   The man the authorities came to blame
   For somethin' that he never done.
   Put in a prison cell, but one time he coulda been
   The champion of the world.

6. Four months later, the ghettoes are in flame.
   Rubin's in South America, fightin' for his name,
   While Arthur Dexter Bradley's still in the robbery game.
   And the cops are puttin' the screws to him, lookin' for
   Somebody to blame.
   "Remember that murder that happened in a bar?"
   "Remember you said you saw the getaway car?"
   "You think you'd like to play ball with the law?"
   "Think it mighta been that fighter that you saw
   Runnin' that night?"
   "Don't forget that you are white."

7. Arthur Dexter Bradley said, "I'm really not sure."
   The cop said, "A poor boy like you could use a break.
   We got you for the motel job and we're talkin' to
   Your friend Bello.
   You don't wanna have to go back to jail; be a nice fellow.
   You'll be doin' society a favor.
   That sonofabitch is brave and gettin' braver.
   We want to put his ass in stir.
   We want to pin this triple murder on him.
   He ain't no Gentleman Jim."

8. Rubin could take a man out with just one punch,
   But he never did like to talk about it all that much.
   "It's my work," he'd say, "and I do it for pay,
   And when it's over, just as soon go on my way
   Up to some paradise
   Where the trout streams flow and the air is nice
   And ride a horse along the trail."
   But then they took him to the jailhouse,
   Where they try to turn a man into a mouse.

9. All of Rubin's cards were marked in advance.
   The trial was a pig-circus; he never had a chance.
   The judge made Rubin's witnesses drunkards from the slums.
   To the white folks who watched, he was a revolutionary bum.
   And to the black folks he was just a crazy nigger.
   No one doubted that he pulled the trigger.
   And though they could not produce the gun,
   The D.A. said he was the one who did the deed,
   And the all-white jury agreed.

10. Rubin Carter was falsely tried.
    The crime was murder one. Guess who testified?
    Bello and Bradley, and they both baldly lied,
    And the newspapers, they all went along for the ride.
    How can the life of such a man
    Be in the palm of some fool's hand?
    To see him obviously framed
    Couldn't help but make me feel ashamed to live in a land
    Where justice is a game.

11. Now all the criminals in their coats and their ties
    Are free to drink martinis and watch the sun rise,
    While Rubin sits like Buddha in a ten-foot cell,
    An innocent man in a living hell.
    Yes, that's the story of the Hurricane,
    But it won't be over till they clear his name
    And give him back the time he's done.
    Put in a prison cell, but one time he coulda been
    The champion of the world.

Standard Ukulele

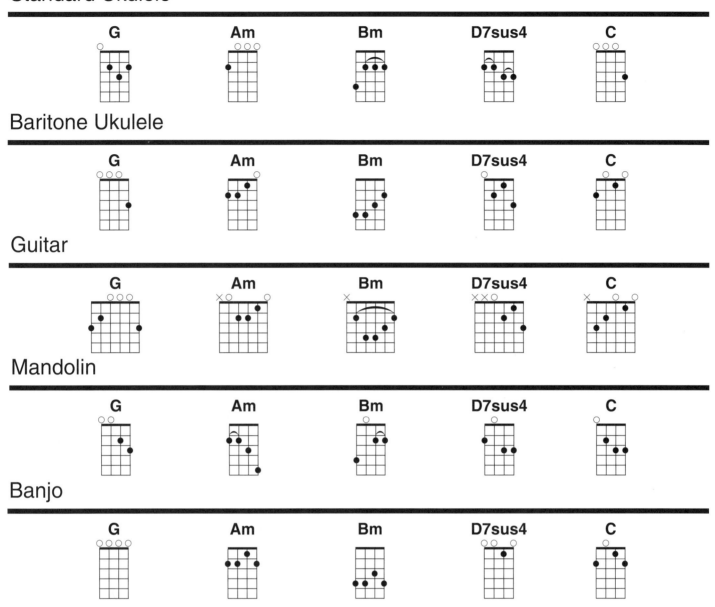

Baritone Ukulele

Guitar

Mandolin

Banjo

I Shall Be Released
Words and Music by Bob Dylan

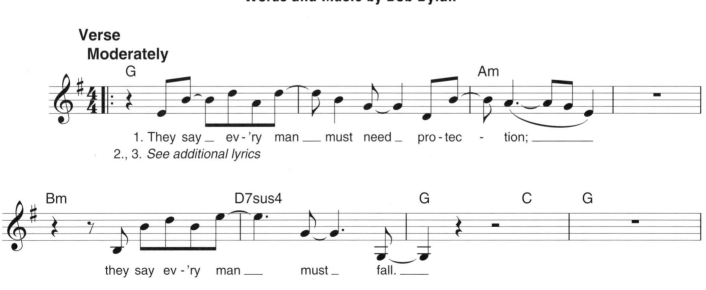

Verse
Moderately

1. They say ev-'ry man must need pro-tec - tion;
2., 3. *See additional lyrics*

they say ev-'ry man must fall.

Yet I ___ swear I see ___ my re - flec - tion

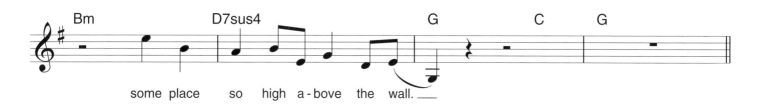

some place so high a - bove the wall. ___

Chorus

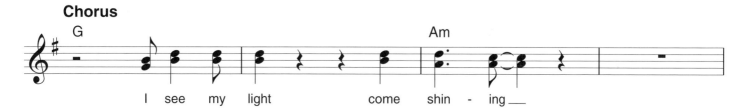

I see my light come shin - ing ___

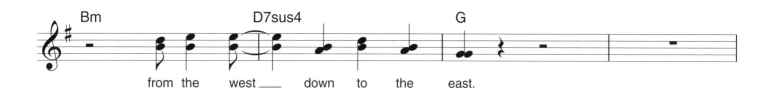

from the west ___ down to the east.

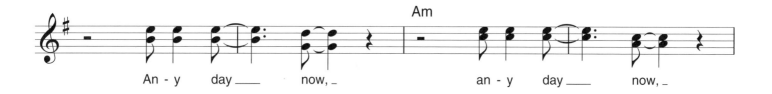

An - y day ___ now, __ an - y day ___ now, __

Play 3 times

I shall ___ be ___ re - leased. __

Additional Lyrics

2. Down here next to me in this lonely crowd
   Is a man who swears he's not to blame.
   All day long I hear him cry so loud,
   Calling out that he's been framed.

3. They say everything can be replaced,
   Yet every distance is not near.
   So I remember every face
   Of every man who put me here.

Standard Ukulele

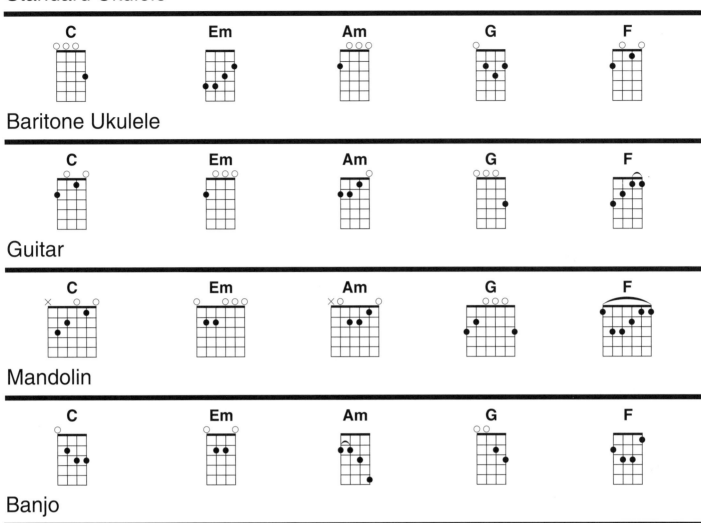

Baritone Ukulele

Guitar

Mandolin

Banjo

I Want You
Words and Music by Bob Dylan

%Verse
Moderately, in 2

C   Em

1. The guilt - y un - der - tak - er sighs, _ the lone - some or - gan
2., 3., 4. *See additional lyrics*

Am   G

grind - er cries, _ the sil - ver sax - o - phones _ say I _ should re - fuse you. _

Additional Lyrics

2. The drunken politician leaps
Upon the street where mothers weep,
And the saviors who are fast asleep,
They wait for you.
And I wait for them to interrupt
Me drinkin' from my broken cup
And ask me to
Open up the gate for you.

3. Well, I return to the Queen of Spades
And talk with my chambermaid.
She knows that I'm not afraid
To look at her.
She is good to me
And there's nothing she doesn't see.
She knows where I'd like to be,
But it doesn't matter.

4. Now your dancing child with his
Chinese suit,
He spoke to me, I took his flute.
No, I wasn't very cute to him, was I?
But I did it because he lied,
And because he took you for a ride
And because time was on his side
And because I...

Standard Ukulele

Baritone Ukulele

Guitar

Mandolin

Banjo

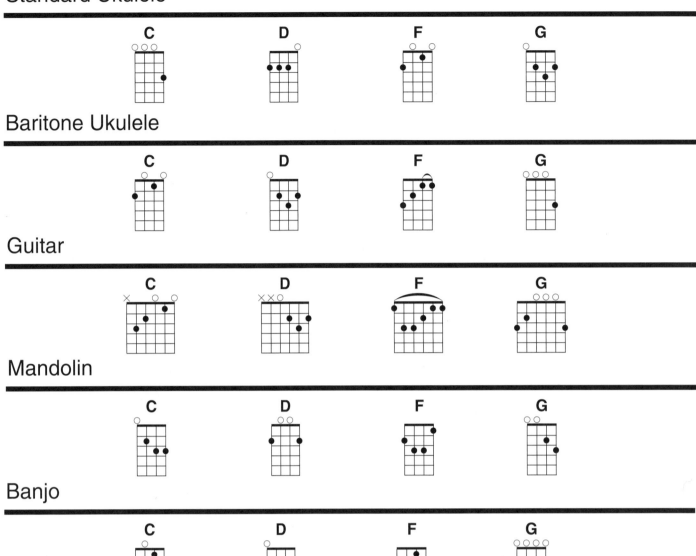

I'll Be Your Baby Tonight

Words and Music by Bob Dylan

1. Close your eyes, _____ close the door. ___
   shut the shade. ___

You don't have to wor - ry _____ an - y - more. ___ }
You don't have _____ to be a - fraid. ___ }

Standard Ukulele

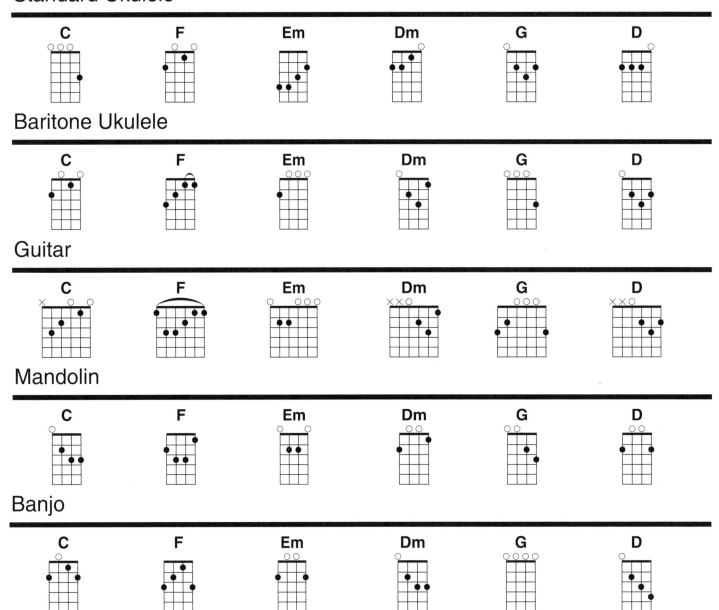

Baritone Ukulele

Guitar

Mandolin

Banjo

If Not for You
Words and Music by Bob Dylan

Moderately   Verse

1. If not for you, _____ babe, I could-n't find the door, _
_____ babe, I'd lay a-wake all night, _

could-n't e-ven see the floor. _
wait for the morn-in' light _

I'd _____ be sad and blue _____
to shine in through, _

Standard Ukulele

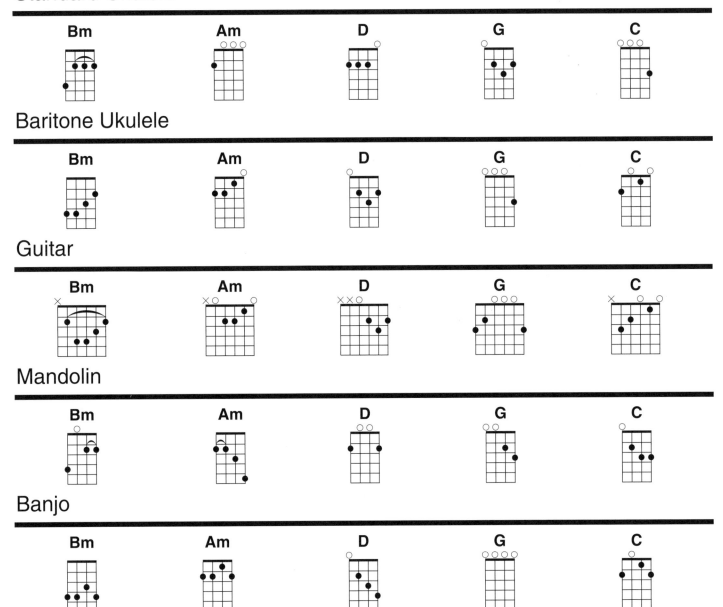

Baritone Ukulele

Guitar

Mandolin

Banjo

It Ain't Me, Babe

Words and Music by Bob Dylan

Verse
Moderately

1. Go 'way from my win-dow, leave at your own cho-sen speed.
2., 3. *See additional lyrics*

I'm not the one you want, babe; I'm not the one you __

need.   You say you're look-in'   for some-one   who's nev-er

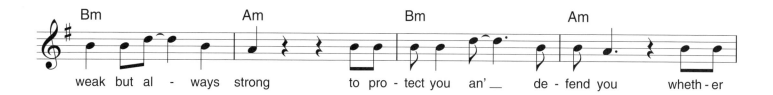

weak but al - ways strong   to pro - tect you   an' __   de - fend you   wheth - er

you are   right   or   wrong,   some - one to   o - pen each and   ev - 'ry

Chorus

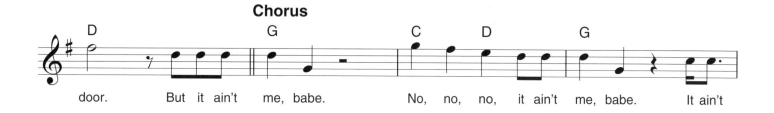

door.   But it ain't   me, babe.   No,   no,   no,   it ain't   me, babe.   It ain't

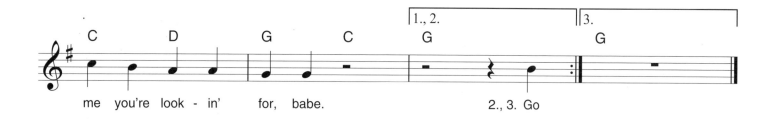

me you're look - in'   for, babe.   2., 3. Go

Additional Lyrics

2. Go lightly from the ledge, babe,
   Go lightly on the ground.
   I'm not the one you want, babe;
   I will only let you down.
   You say you're lookin' for someone
   Who will promise never to part,
   Someone to close his eyes for you,
   Someone to close his heart,
   Someone who will die for you and more.

3. Go melt back into the night, babe;
   Everything inside is made of stone.
   There's nothing in here moving,
   And anyway, I'm not alone.
   You say you're lookin' for someone
   Who'll pick you up each time you fall,
   To gather flowers constantly
   And to come each time you call,
   A lover for your life and nothing more.

Standard Ukulele

Baritone Ukulele

Guitar

Mandolin

Banjo

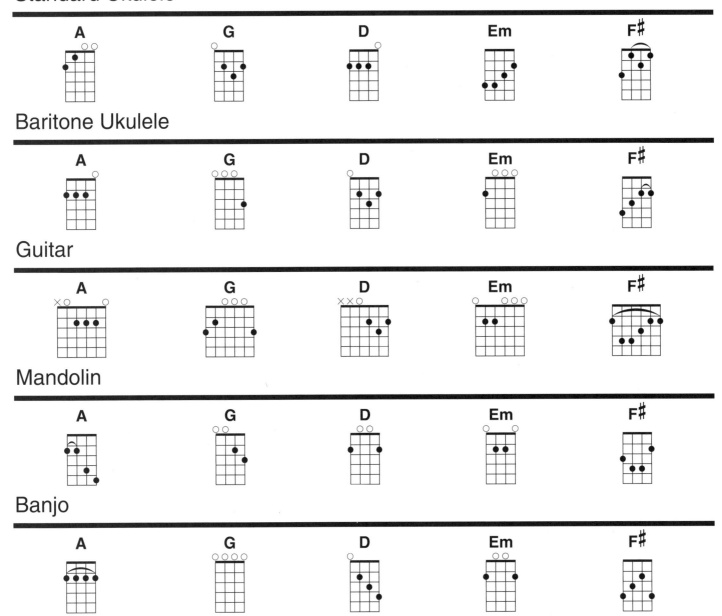

It's All Over Now, Baby Blue

Words and Music by Bob Dylan

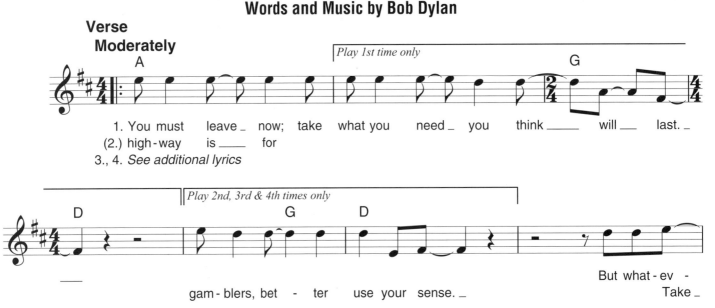

Verse
Moderately

Play 1st time only

1. You must leave now; take what you need you think will last.
(2.) high-way is for
3., 4. *See additional lyrics*

Play 2nd, 3rd & 4th times only

gam - blers, bet - ter use your sense.

But what - ev -
Take

Additional Lyrics

3. All your seasick sailors, they are rowing home.
Your empty-handed army is all going home.
Your lover who just walked out the door
Has taken all his blankets from the floor.
The carpet, too, is moving under you,
And it's all over now, Baby Blue.

4. Leave your stepping stones behind,now something calls for you.
Forget the dead you've left,they will not follow you.
The vagabond who's rapping at your door
Is standing in the clothes that you once wore.
Strike another match, go start anew,
And it's all over now, Baby Blue.

Standard Ukulele

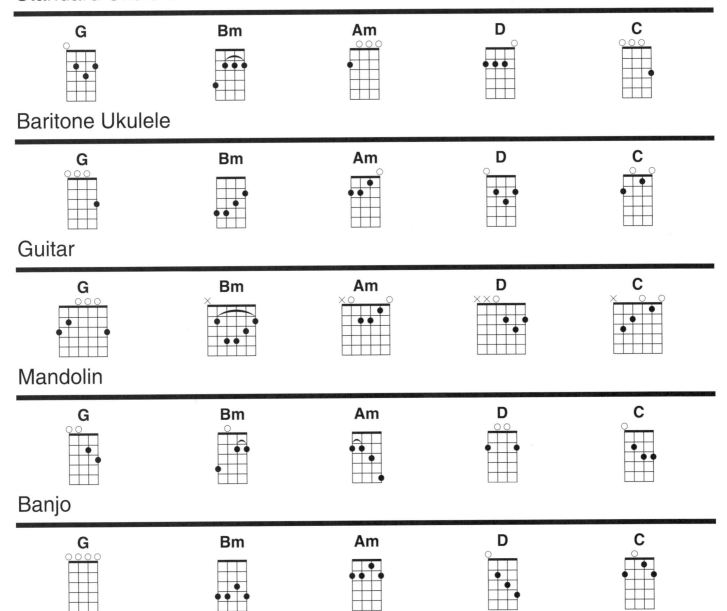

Baritone Ukulele

Guitar

Mandolin

Banjo

Jokerman
Words and Music by Bob Dylan

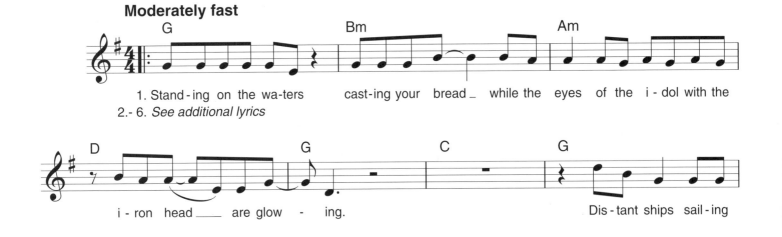

Verse
Moderately fast

1. Stand-ing on the wa-ters cast-ing your bread __ while the eyes of the i - dol with the
2.- 6. *See additional lyrics*

i - ron head ____ are glow - ing.

Dis - tant ships sail - ing

Additional Lyrics

2. So swiftly the sun sets in the sky.
   You rise up and say goodbye to no one.
   Fools rush in where angels fear to tread.
   Both of their futures, so full of dread, you
   Don't show one.
   Shedding off one more layer of skin,
   Keeping one step ahead of the
   Persecutor within.

3. You're a man of the mountains; you can
   Walk on the clouds.
   Manipulator of crowds, you're a dream twister.
   You're going to Sodom and Gomorrah,
   But what do you care? Ain't nobody there
   would want to marry your sister.
   Friend to the martyr, a friend to the woman
   Of shame,
   You look into the fiery furnace, see the rich man
   Without any name.

4. Well, the Book of Leviticus and Deuteronomy,
   The law of the jungle and the sea are your
   Only teachers.
   In the smoke of the twilight on a milk-white steed,
   Michelangelo indeed could've carved out
   Your features.
   Resting in the fields, far from the turbulent space,
   Half asleep near the stars with a small dog
   Licking your face.

5. Well, the rifleman's stalking the sick and the lame.
   Preacherman seeks the same; who'll get there
   First is uncertain.
   Nightsticks and water cannons, tear gas, padlocks,
   Molotov cocktails and rocks behind every curtain.
   False-hearted judges dying in the webs that they spin.
   Only a matter of time till night comes steppin' in.

6. It's a shadowy world; skies are slippery gray.
   A woman just gave birth to a prince today and
   Dressed him in scarlet.
   He'll put the priest in his pocket, put the blade to
   The heat,
   Take the motherless children off the street and place
   Them at the feet of a harlot.
   Oh, Jokerman, you know what he wants.
   Oh, Jokerman, you don't show any response.

Standard Ukulele

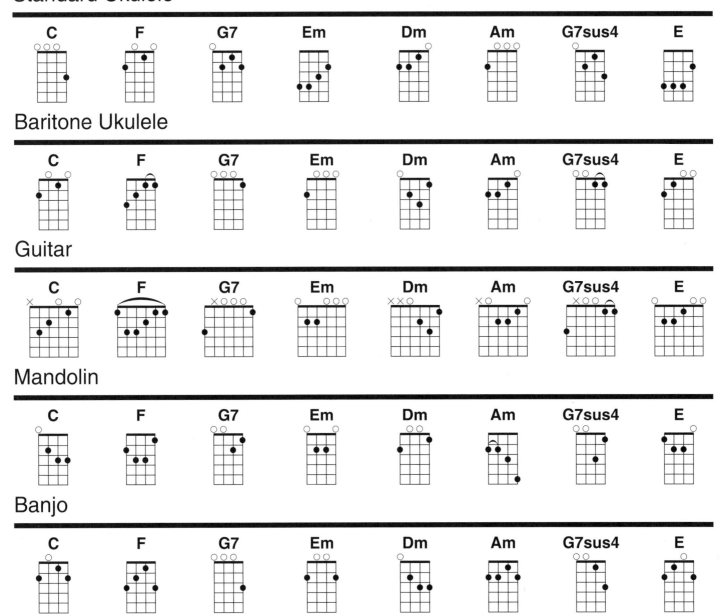

Baritone Ukulele

Guitar

Mandolin

Banjo

Just Like a Woman
Words and Music by Bob Dylan

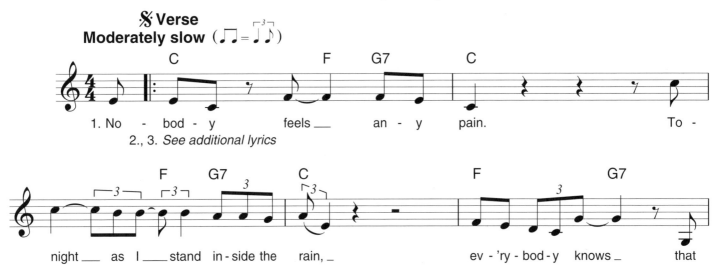

% **Verse**
Moderately slow

1. No - bod - y feels ___ an - y pain. To -
2., 3. *See additional lyrics*

night ___ as I ___ stand in - side the rain, ___ ev - 'ry - bod - y knows ___ that

Additional Lyrics

2. Queen Mary, she's my friend.
   Yes, I believe I'll go see her again.
   Nobody has to guess that Baby can't be blessed
   Till she finally sees that she's like all the rest,
   With her fog, her amphetamine and her pearls.

3. I just can't fit.
   Yes, I believe it's time for us to quit.
   When we meet again, introduced as friends.
   Please don't let on that you knew me when
   I was hungry and it was your world.

Chorus 2. She takes just like a woman, yes.
   She makes love just like a woman; yes, she does.
   And she aches just like a woman,
   But she breaks just like a little girl.

Chorus 3. Ah, you fake just like a woman; yes, you do.
   You make love just like a woman; yes, you do.
   Then you ache just like a woman,
   But you break just like a little girl.

Standard Ukulele

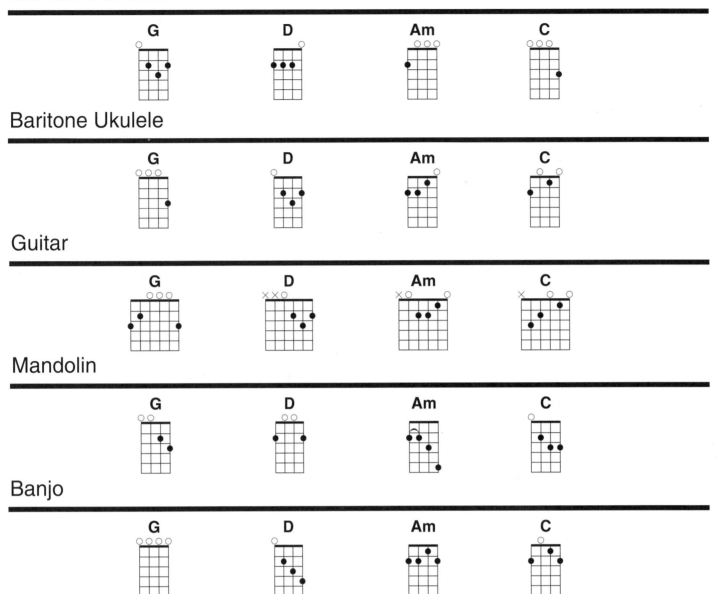

Baritone Ukulele

Guitar

Mandolin

Banjo

Knockin' on Heaven's Door
Words and Music by Bob Dylan

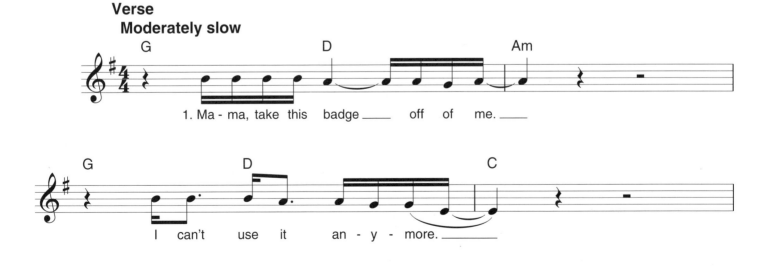

Verse
Moderately slow

1. Ma - ma, take this badge _____ off of me. _____

I can't use it an - y - more. _____

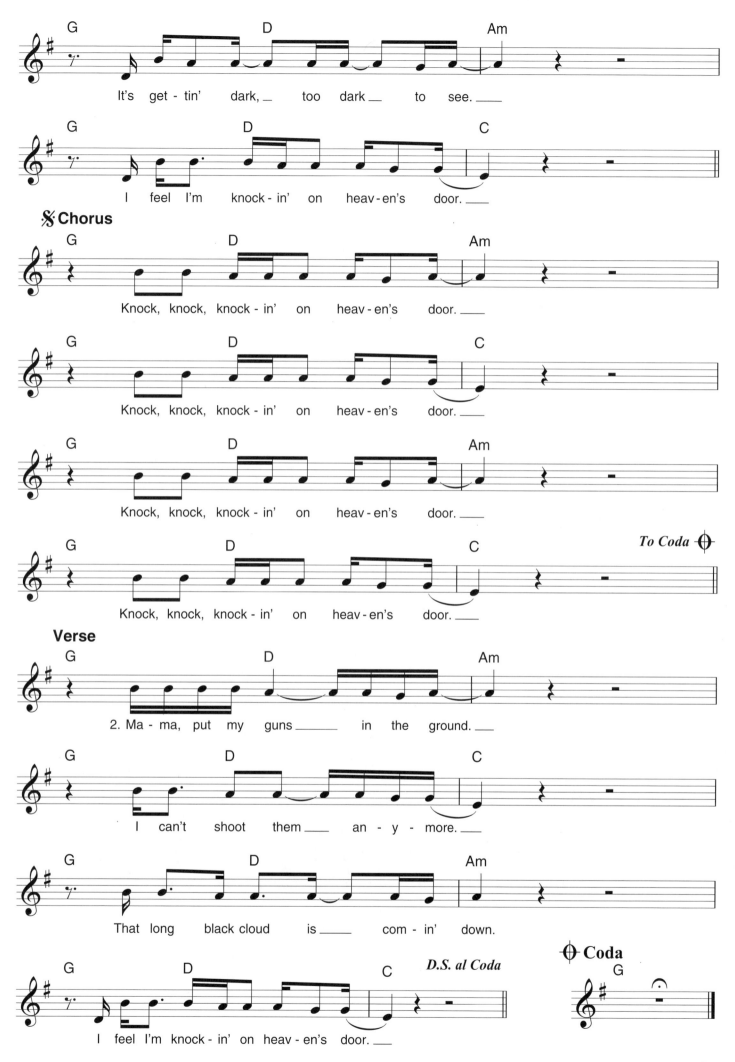

Standard Ukulele

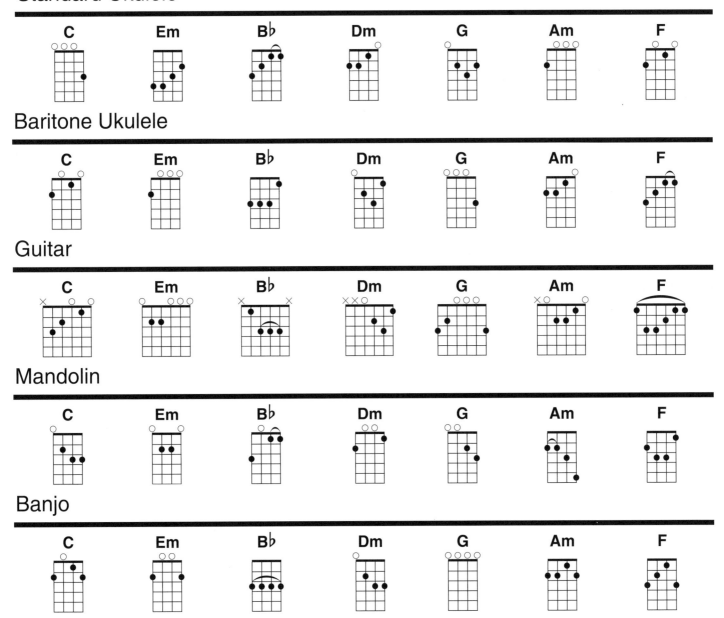

Baritone Ukulele

Guitar

Mandolin

Banjo

Lay, Lady, Lay
Words and Music by Bob Dylan

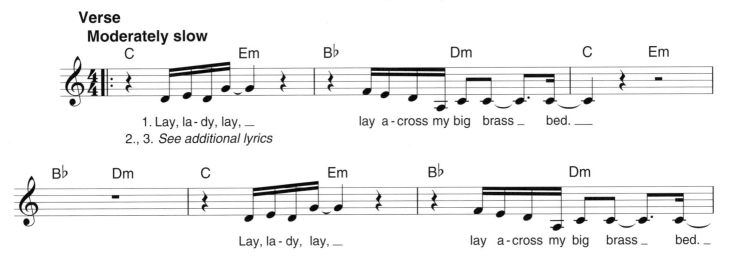

Verse
Moderately slow

1. Lay, la-dy, lay, _ lay a-cross my big brass _ bed. _
2., 3. *See additional lyrics*

Lay, la-dy, lay, _ lay a-cross my big brass _ bed. _

Additional Lyrics

2. Stay, lady, stay, stay with your man awhile,
   Until the break of day; let me see you make him smile.
   His clothes are dirty but his hands are clean,
   And you're the best thing that he's ever seen.
   Stay, lady, stay, stay with your man awhile.

3. Lay, lady, lay, lay across my big brass bed.
   Stay, lady, stay, stay while the night is still ahead.
   I long to see you in the morning light.
   I long to reach for you in the night.
   Stay, lady, stay, stay while the night is still ahead.

Standard Ukulele

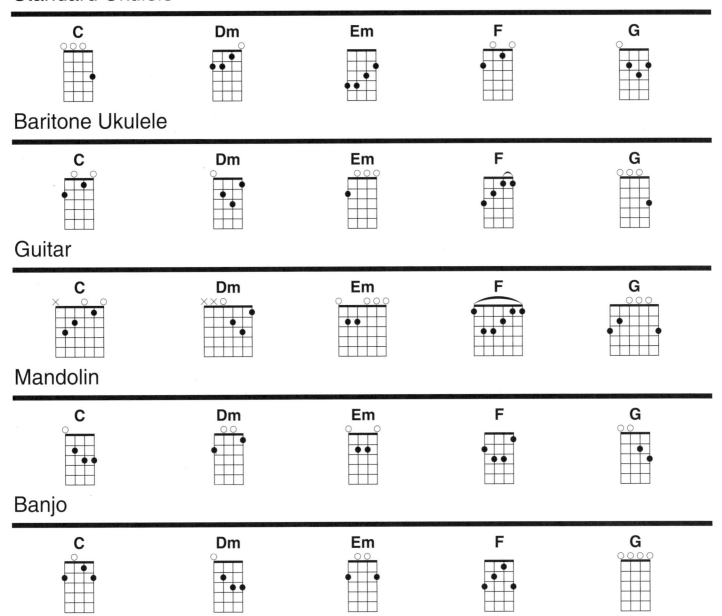

Baritone Ukulele

Guitar

Mandolin

Banjo

Like a Rolling Stone
Words and Music by Bob Dylan

Verse
Moderately

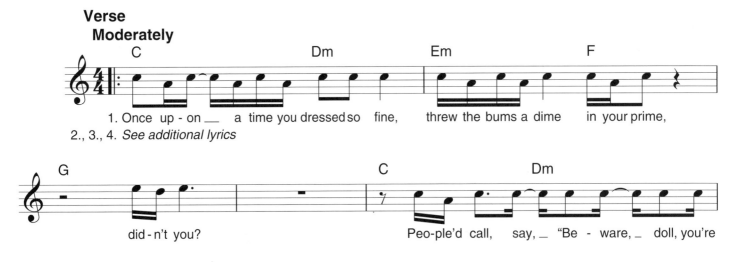

1. Once up - on ___ a time you dressed so fine, threw the bums a dime in your prime,
2., 3., 4. *See additional lyrics*

did - n't you? Peo-ple'd call, say, ___ "Be - ware, ___ doll, you're

Chorus

Additional Lyrics

2. Oh, you've gone to the finest school all right, Miss Lonely,
But you know you only used to get juiced in it.
Nobody's ever taught you how to live out on the street,
And now you're gonna have to get used to it.
You say you never compromise with the mystery tramp,
But now you realize he's not selling any alibis
As you stare into the vacuum of his eyes
And say, "Do you want to make a deal?"

3. Oh, you never turned around to see the frowns
On the jugglers and the clowns when they all did tricks for you.
You never understood that it ain't no good;
You shouldn't let other people get your kicks for you.
You used to ride on the chrome horse with your diplomat
Who carried on his shoulder a Siamese cat.
Ain't it hard when you discover that he really wasn't where it's at,
After he took from you everything he could steal?

4. Oh, princess on the steeple and all the pretty people,
They're all drinking, thinking that they got it made.
Exchanging all precious gifts, but you better take
Your diamond ring.
You'd better pawn it, babe.
You used to be so amused at Napoleon in rags
And the language that he used.
Go to him now; he calls you. You can't refuse.
When you ain't got nothing, you got nothing to lose.
You're invisible now; you got no secrets to conceal.

Standard Ukulele

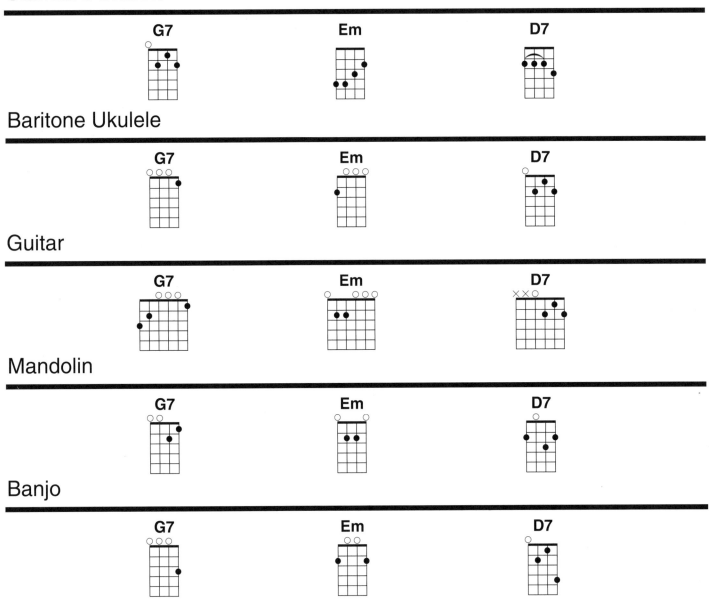

Baritone Ukulele

Guitar

Mandolin

Banjo

Maggie's Farm
Words and Music by Bob Dylan

Verse
Moderately fast

1. I ain't gon - na work ___ on Mag - gie's farm ___ no more.
2.- 5. *See additional lyrics*

No, I ain't gon - na work ___ on Mag - gie's farm ___

___ no more.   Well, I   wake up   in ___ the morn-

- ing,   fold   my   hands   and pray   for   rain. _____   I   got a

head   full   of ___ i - deas ___   that are driv - in'   me ___ in - sane. __

___   It's   a   shame ___   the   way ___   she   makes ___ me   scrub ___ the   floor. __

D7   G7

___   I _____   ain't gon - na   work ___ on   Mag - gie's   farm __

___   no   more.   2.- 5. I

Additional Lyrics

2. I ain't gonna work for Maggie's brother no more.
   No, I ain't gonna work for Maggie's brother no more.
   Well, he hands you a nickel, he hands you a dime,
   He asks you with a grin if you're havin' a good time.
   Then he fines you every time you slam the door.
   I ain't gonna work for Maggie's brother no more.

3. I ain't gonna work for Maggie's pa no more.
   No, I ain't gonna work for Maggie's pa no more.
   Well, he puts his cigar out in your face just for kicks.
   His bedroom window, it is made out of bricks.
   The National Guard stands around his door.
   Ah, I ain't gonna work for Maggie's pa no more.

4. I ain't gonna work for Maggie's ma no more.
   No, I ain't gonna work for Maggie's ma no more.
   Well, she talks to all the servants about man
   And God and law.
   Everybody says she's the brains behind pa.
   She's sixty-eight, but she says she's fifty-four.
   I ain't gonna work for Maggie's ma no more.

5. I ain't gonna work on Maggie's farm no more.
   I ain't gonna work on Maggie's farm no more.
   Well, I try my best to be just like I am,
   But everybody wants you to be just like them.
   They say sing while you slave and I just get bored.
   I ain't gonna work on Maggie's farm no more.

Standard Ukulele

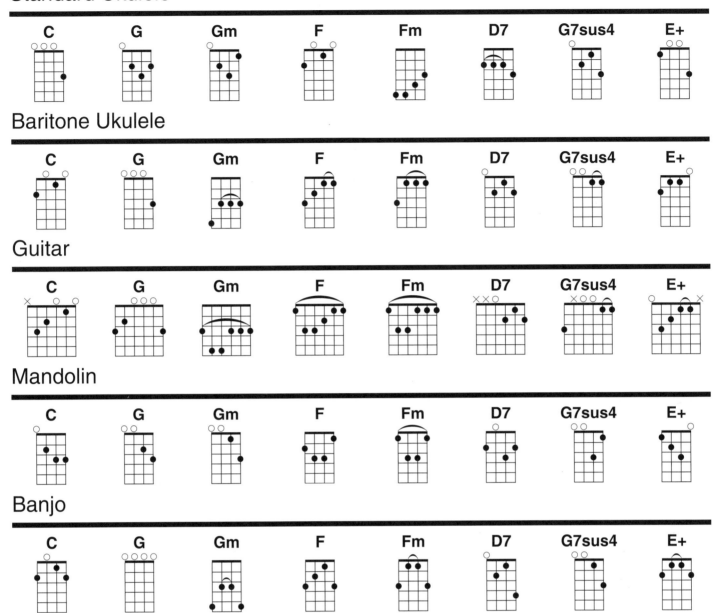

Baritone Ukulele

Guitar

Mandolin

Banjo

Make You Feel My Love

Words and Music by Bob Dylan

Verse
Moderately slow

1. When the rain __ is blow - ing in your face
2. When eve - ning shad - ows and the stars ap - pear

and the whole __ world is on your case, __
and there is no ___ one there to dry your tears, __

I could of - fer you a
I could hold __ you for a

Standard Ukulele

Baritone Ukulele

Guitar

Mandolin

Banjo

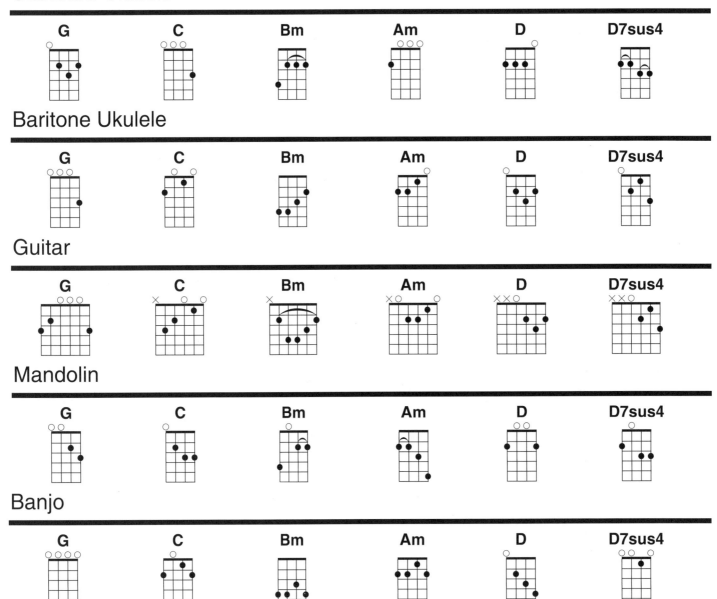

The Man in Me
Words and Music by Bob Dylan

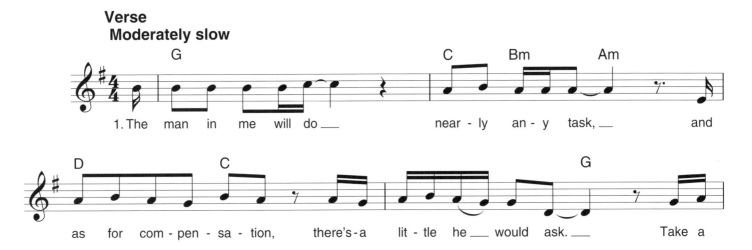

Verse
Moderately slow

1. The man in me will do ___ near-ly an-y task, ___ and as for com-pen-sa-tion, there's-a lit-tle he ___ would ask. ___ Take a

Standard Ukulele

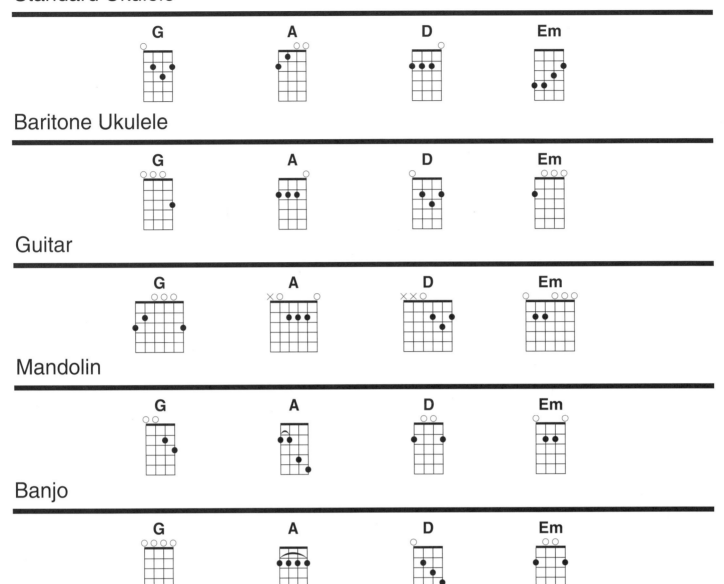

Baritone Ukulele

Guitar

Mandolin

Banjo

Mr. Tambourine Man
Words and Music by Bob Dylan

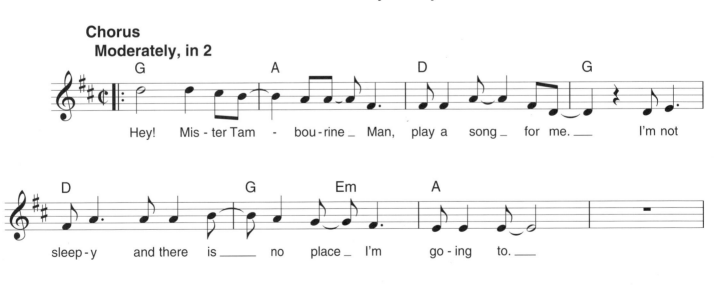

Chorus
Moderately, in 2

G   A   D   G

Hey! Mis - ter Tam - bou - rine _ Man, play a song _ for me. _ I'm not

D   G   Em   A

sleep - y and there is _____ no place _ I'm go - ing to. _____

Additional Lyrics

2. Take me on a trip upon your magic swirlin' ship.
My senses have been stripped, my hands
Can't feel to grip,
My toes too numb to step.
Wait only for my boot heels to be wanderin'.
I'm ready to go anywhere, I'm ready for to fade
Into my own parade; cast your dancing spell my way.
I promise to go under it.

3. Though you might hear laughin', spinnin', swingin'
Madly across the sun,
It's not aimed at anyone; it's just escapin' on the run,
And but for the sky there are no fences facin'.
And if you hear vague traces of skippin' reels of rhyme
To your tambourine in time, it's just a ragged
Clown behind.
I wouldn't pay it any mind.
It's just a shadow you're seein' that he's chasing.

4. Then take me disappearin' through the smoke
Rings of my mind,
Down the foggy ruins of time, far past the
Frozen leaves,
The haunted, frightened trees, out to the
Windy beach,
Far from the twisted reach of crazy sorrow.
Yes, to dance beneath the diamond sky with one
Hand waving free,
Silhouetted by the sea, circled by the circus sands
With all memory and fate driven deep beneath
The waves.
Let me forget about today until tomorrow.

Standard Ukulele

Baritone Ukulele

Guitar

Mandolin

Banjo

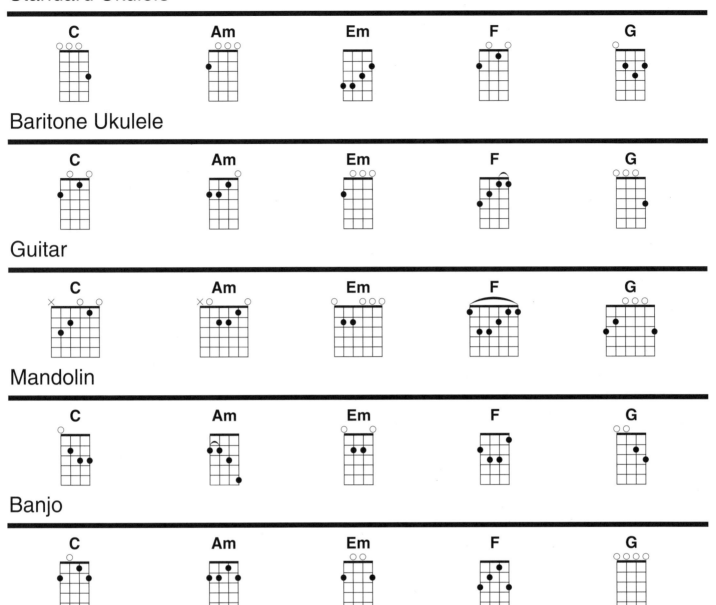

My Back Pages
Words and Music by Bob Dylan

Verse
Moderately

1. Crim - son ____ flames ____ tied through my ____ ears, ____ roll - in'
2. – 6. *See additional lyrics*

high and might - y _____ traps. ____ Pounced with

fire ___ on ___ flam-ing roads, ___ us-ing i - deas _ as my
maps. ___ "We'll meet on _____ edg - es
soon," said _ I, _____ proud 'neath heat - ed brow. ___
___ Ah, but I was so much old - er then; ___ I'm
young - er ___ than ___ that now. ___

1. 2., 3. 4. 5. 6.

3. Girls' 5. In a 6. Yes, my
4. A

Additional Lyrics

2. Half-wracked prejudice leaped forth.
"Rip down all hate," I screamed.
Lies that life is black and white
Spoke from my skull. I dreamed
Romantic facts of musketeers,
Foundationed deep, somehow.
Ah, but I was so much older then;
I'm younger than that now.

3. Girls' faces formed the forward path
From phony jealousy
To memorizing politics
Of ancient history,
Flung down by corpse evangelists
Unthought of, though, somehow.
Ah, but I was so much older then;
I'm younger than that now.

4. A self-ordained professor's tongue
Too serious to fool
Spouted out that liberty
Is just equality in school.
"Equality," I spoke the word
As if a wedding vow.
Ah, but I was so much older then;
I'm younger than that now.

5. In a soldier's stance, I aimed my hand
At the mongrel dogs who teach,
Fearing not that I'd become my enemy
In the instant that I preach.
My existence led by confusion boats,
Mutiny from stern to bow.
Ah, but I was so much older then;
I'm younger than that now.

6. Yes, my guard stood hard when abstract threats,
Too noble to neglect,
Deceived me into thinking
I had something to protect.
Good and bad, I define these terms,
Quite clear, no doubt, somehow.
Ah, but I was so much older then;
I'm younger than that now.

Standard Ukulele

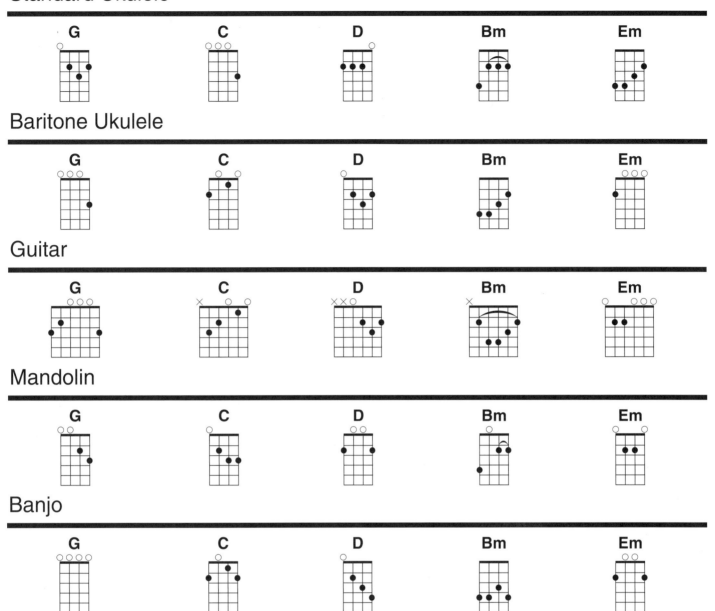

Baritone Ukulele

Guitar

Mandolin

Banjo

Not Dark Yet
Words and Music by Bob Dylan

Verse
Slowly, in 2

1. Shad-ows are fall - ing and I've been here all day.
2., 3., 4. *See additional lyrics*

It's too hot to sleep,

time is run-ning a - way. ___   Feel like my soul ___

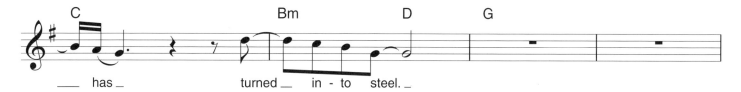

___ has ___   turned ___ in - to   steel. _

I've still got the scars ___   that the sun _____ did - n't heal. ___

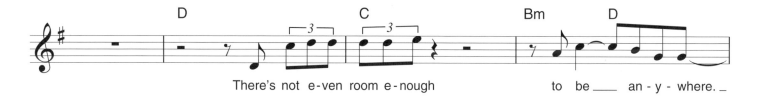

There's not e-ven room e - nough   to be ___ an - y - where. _

It's not dark   yet,

Play 4 times

but it's ___ get - ting there. _

Additional Lyrics

2. Well, my sense of humanity has gone down the drain.
   Behind every beautiful thing there's been some kind of pain.
   She wrote me a letter and she wrote it so kind.
   She put down in writing what was in her mind.
   I just don't see why I should even care.
   It's not dark yet, but it's getting there.

3. Well, I've been to London and I've been to gay Paree.
   I've followed the river and I got to the sea.
   I've been down on the bottom of a world full of lies.
   I ain't looking for nothing in anyone's eyes.
   Sometimes my burden seems more than I can bear.
   It's not dark yet, but it's getting there.

4. I was born here and I'll die here against my will.
   I know it looks like I'm moving, but I'm standing still.
   Every nerve in my body is so vacant and numb.
   I can't even remember what it was I came here to get away from.
   Don't even hear a murmur of a prayer.
   It's not dark yet, but it's getting there.

Standard Ukulele

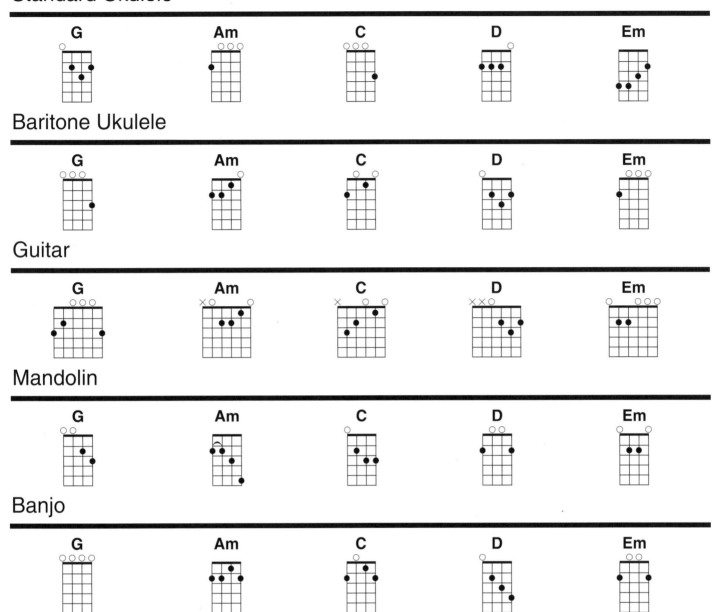

Baritone Ukulele

Guitar

Mandolin

Banjo

Positively 4th Street

Words and Music by Bob Dylan

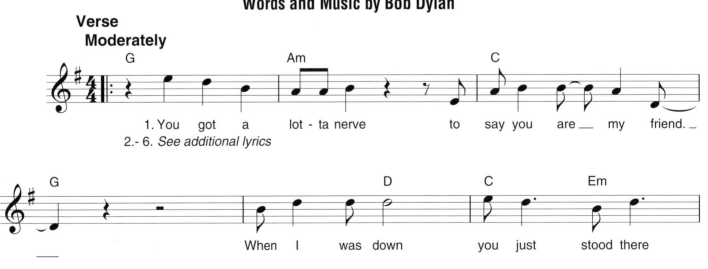

Verse
Moderately

1. You got a lot-ta nerve to say you are __ my friend. __
2.- 6. *See additional lyrics*

When I was down you just stood there

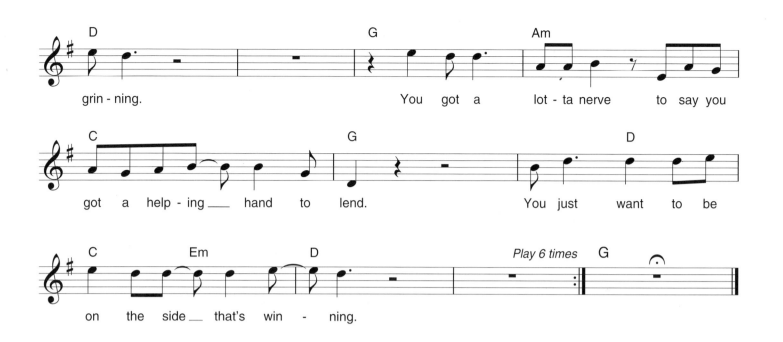

grin - ning.

You got a lot - ta nerve to say you got a help - ing ___ hand to lend. You just want to be on the side ___ that's win - ning.

Play 6 times

Additional Lyrics

2. You say I let you down;
   You know it's not like that.
   If you're so hurt,
   Why, then, don't you show it?
   You say you lost your faith,
   But that's not where it's at.
   You have no faith to lose
   And you know it.

3. I know the reason
   That you talk behind my back.
   I used to be among the crowd
   You're in with.
   Do you take me for such a fool
   To think I'd make contact
   With the one who tries to hide
   What he don't know to begin with?

4. You see me on the street,
   You always act surprised.
   You say, "How are you? Good luck,"
   But you don't mean it.
   When you know as well as me
   You'd rather see me paralyzed,
   Why don't you just come out once
   And scream it?

5. No, I do not feel that good
   When I see the heartbreaks you embrace.
   If I was a master thief,
   Perhaps I'd rob them.
   And now I know you're dissatisfied
   With your position and your place.
   Don't you understand
   It's not my problem?

6. I wish that for just one time
   You could stand inside my shoes
   And just for that one moment
   I could be you.
   Yes, I wish that for just one time
   You could stand inside my shoes.
   You'd know what a drag it is
   To see you.

Standard Ukulele

Baritone Ukulele

Guitar

Mandolin

Banjo

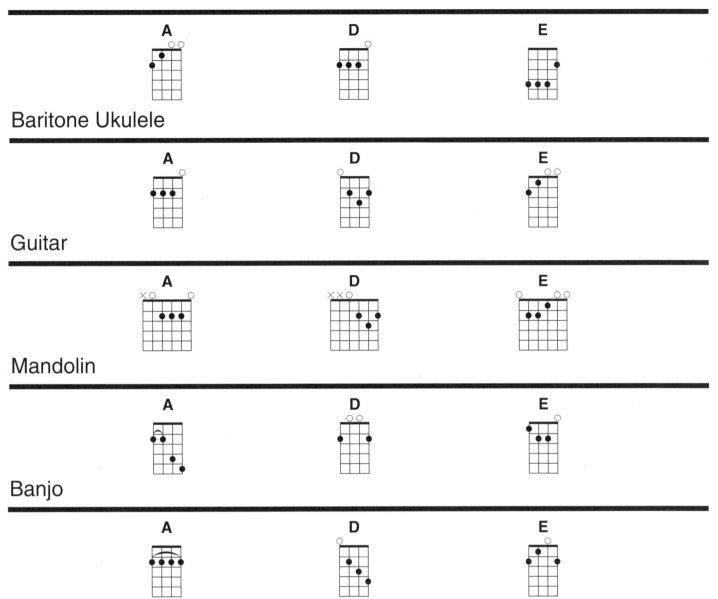

Quinn, the Eskimo (The Mighty Quinn)
Words and Music by Bob Dylan

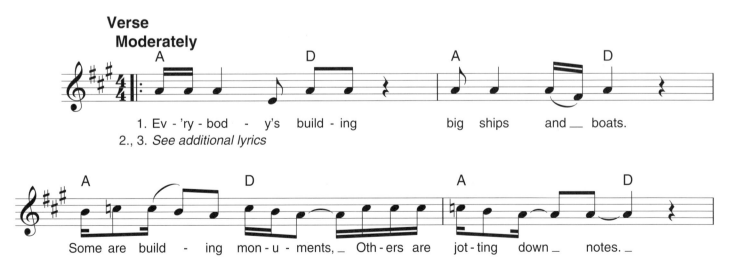

1. Ev - 'ry - bod - y's build - ing big ships and __ boats.
2., 3. *See additional lyrics*

Some are build - ing mon - u - ments, __ Oth - ers are jot - ting down __ notes. __

Additional Lyrics

2. Now, I like to go just like the rest;
   I like my sugar sweet.
   But guarding fumes and making haste,
   It ain't my cup of meat.
   Everybody's here standin' 'round 'neath the trees,
   Feeding pigeons on a limb.
   But when Quinn, the Eskimo, gets here,
   Them pigeons are gonna go to him.

3. Now, lamp-gate and gunney-dew,
   I can recite 'em all.
   Just tell me where to put 'em
   And I'll tell you who to call.
   Now, nobody can get any sleep;
   There's someone on everybody's toes.
   But when Quinn, the Eskimo, gets here,
   Everybody's gonna doze.

Standard Ukulele

Baritone Ukulele

Guitar

Mandolin

Banjo

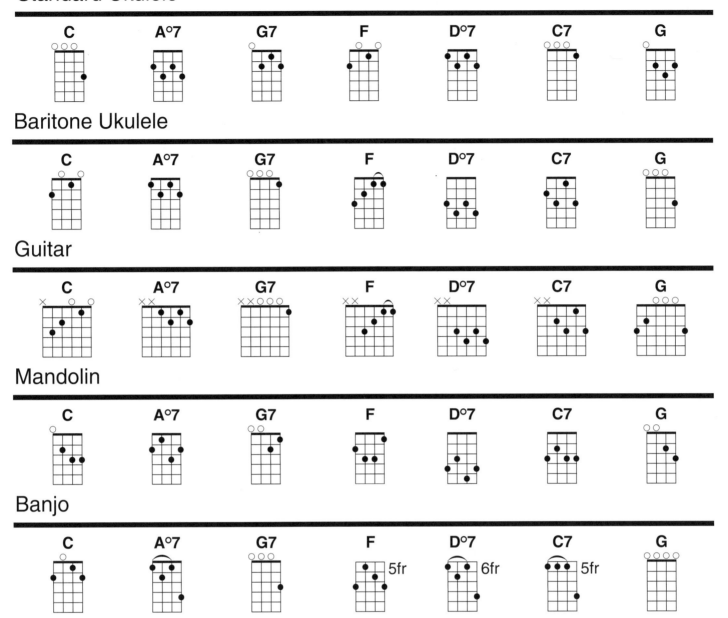

Rainy Day Women # 12 & 35
Words and Music by Bob Dylan

Moderately, in 2

Verse

C   A°7   G7   C

1. Well, __ they'll stone ya when you're try - na be so good. They'll

2.- 5. *See additional lyrics*

A°7   G7   C

stone ya just like ____ they said they would. They'll

1.- 4.

5.

Additional Lyrics

2. Well, they'll stone ya when you're walkin' on the street.
   They'll stone ya when you're tryna keep your seat.
   They'll stone ya when you're walkin' on the floor.
   They'll stone ya when you're walkin' through the door.
   But I would not feel so all alone,
   Everybody must get stoned.

3. They'll stone ya when you're at the breakfast table.
   They'll stone ya when you are young and able.
   They'll stone ya when you're tryna make a buck.
   They'll stone ya and then they'll say, "Good luck."
   Yeah, but I would not feel so all alone,
   Everybody must get stoned.

4. Well, they'll stone you and say that it's the end.
   Then they'll stone you and then they'll come back again.
   They'll stone you when you're riding in your car.
   They'll stone you when you're playing your guitar.
   Yes, but I would not feel so all alone,
   Everybody must get stoned.

5. Well, they'll stone you when you walk all alone.
   They'll stone you when you are walking home.
   They'll stone you and then say you are brave.
   They'll stone you when you're set down in your grave.
   But I would not feel so all alone,
   Everybody must get stoned.

Standard Ukulele

Baritone Ukulele

Guitar

Mandolin

Banjo

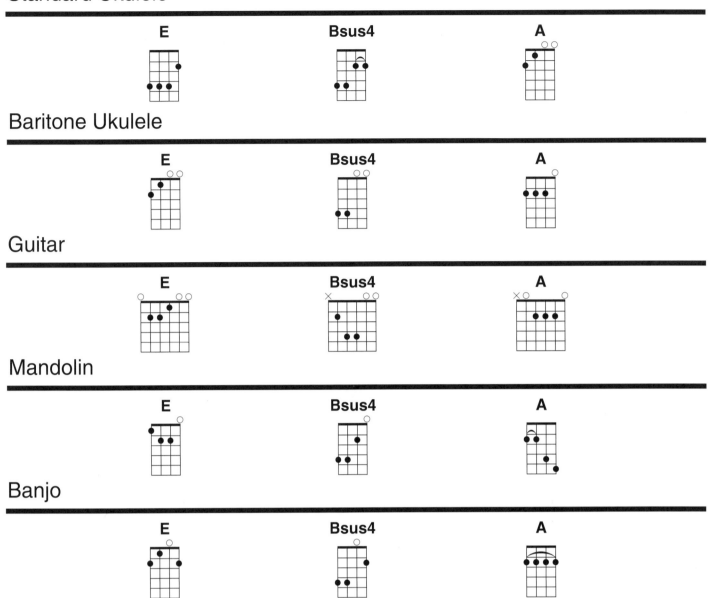

Shelter from the Storm
Words and Music by Bob Dylan

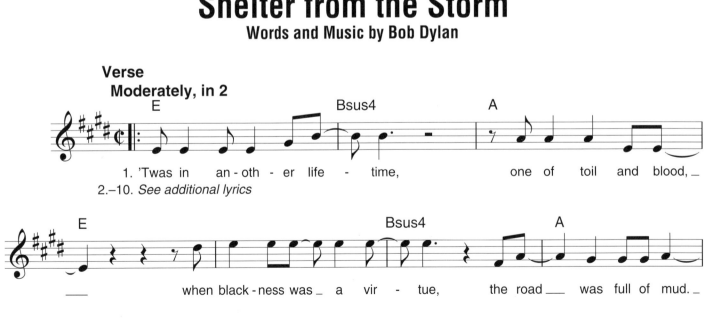

Verse
Moderately, in 2

1. 'Twas in an - oth - er life - time, one of toil and blood, __
2.–10. *See additional lyrics*

__ when black - ness was __ a vir - tue, the road __ was full of mud. __

I came in from the wil - der - ness, a crea - ture void _ of form. _

"Come in," she said, "I'll give _ ya shel ter from _ the

storm."

2. And

Additional Lyrics

2. And if I pass this way again, you can rest assured
   I'll always do my best for her; on that I give my word.
   In a world of steel-eyed death and men who are fighting to be warm,
   "Come in," she said, "I'll give ya shelter from the storm."

3. Not a word was spoke between us; there was little risk involved.
   Everything up to that point had been left unresolved.
   Try imagining a place where it's always safe and warm.
   "Come in," she said, "I'll give ya shelter from the storm."

4. I was burned out from exhaustion, buried in the hail,
   Poisoned in the bushes and blown out on the trail,
   Hunted like a crocodile, ravaged in the corn.
   "Come in," she said, "I'll give ya shelter from the storm."

5. Suddenly, I turned around and she was standin' there
   With silver bracelets on her wrists and flowers in her hair.
   She walked up to me so gracefully and took my crown of thorns.
   "Come in," she said, "I'll give ya shelter from the storm."

6. Now there's a wall between us; somethin' there's been lost.
   I took too much for granted; I got my signals crossed.
   Just to think that it all began on a noneventful morn.
   "Come in," she said, "I'll give ya shelter from the storm."

7. Well, the deputy walks on hard nails and the preacher rides a mount,
   But nothing really matters much; it's doom alone that counts.
   And the one-eyed undertaker, he blows a futile horn.
   "Come in," she said, "I'll give ya shelter from the storm."

8. I've heard newborn babies wailin' like a mournin' dove
   And old men with broken teeth stranded without love.
   Do I understand your question, man? Is it hopeless and forlorn?
   "Come in," she said, "I'll give ya shelter from the storm."

9. In a little hilltop village, they gambled for my clothes.
   I bargained for salvation and she gave me a lethal dose.
   I offered up my innocence; I got repaid with scorn.
   "Come in," she said, "I'll give ya shelter from the storm."

10. Well, I'm livin' in a foreign country, but I'm bound to cross the line.
    Beauty walks a razor's edge; someday I'll make it mine.
    If I could only turn back the clock to when God and her were born.
    "Come in," she said, "I'll give ya shelter from the storm."

Standard Ukulele

Baritone Ukulele

Guitar

Mandolin

Banjo

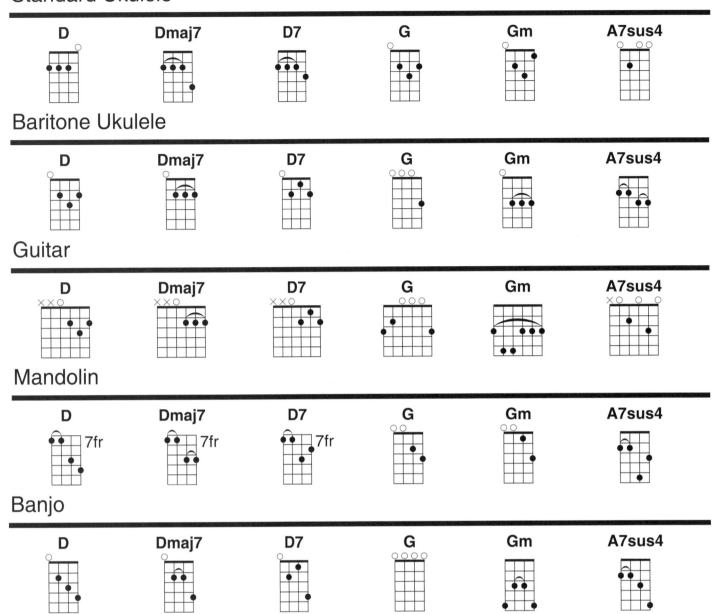

Simple Twist of Fate
Words and Music by Bob Dylan

1. They sat together in the park as the eve-ning sky
2.-6. *See additional lyrics*

grew dark. She looked at him and he felt a spark

tin - gle   to ___ his   bones. ___

'Twas then __ he   felt   a - lone _

___   and wished   that he'd gone   straight _   and

watched out   for   a   sim - ple twist of fate.

Play 6 times

Additional Lyrics

2. They walked along by the old canal,
   A little confused, I remember well,
   And stopped into a strange hotel with a neon burnin' bright.
   He felt the heat of the night hit him like a freight train
   Moving with a simple twist of fate.

3. A saxophone someplace far off played
   As she was walkin' on by the arcade.
   As the light bust through a beat-up shade where he was wakin' up,
   She dropped a coin into the cup of a blind man at the gate
   And forgot about a simple twist of fate.

4. He woke up, the room was bare.
   He didn't see her anywhere.
   He told himself he didn't care, pushed the window open wide,
   Felt an emptiness inside to which he just could not relate,
   Brought on by a simple twist of fate.

5. He hears the ticking of the clocks
   And walks along with a parrot that talks,
   Hunts her down by the waterfront docks where the sailors all come in.
   Maybe she'll pick him out again, how long must he wait
   One more time for a simple twist of fate?

6. People tell me it's a sin
   To know and feel too much within.
   I still believe she was my twin, but I lost the ring.
   She was born in spring, but I was born too late.
   Blame it on a simple twist of fate.

Standard Ukulele

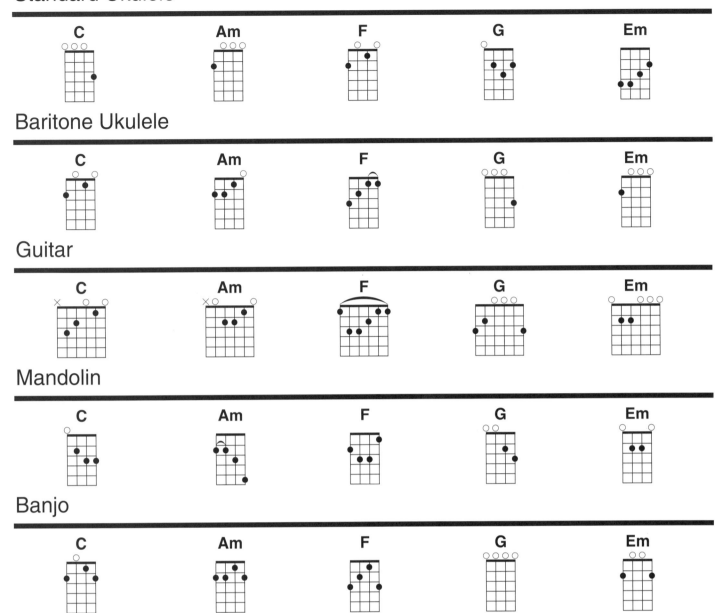

Baritone Ukulele

Guitar

Mandolin

Banjo

Stuck Inside of Mobile with the Memphis Blues Again
Words and Music by Bob Dylan

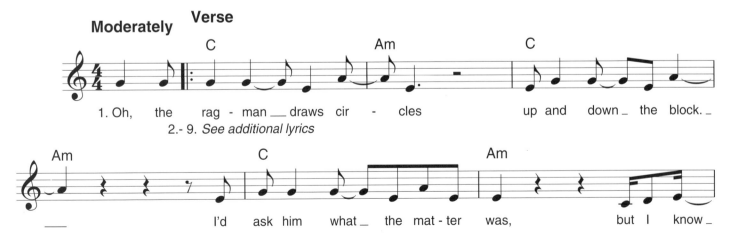

1. Oh, the rag-man draws cir-cles up and down the block.
2.- 9. *See additional lyrics*

I'd ask him what the mat-ter was, but I know

that he don't talk. ___ And the la - dies treat me kind - ly, and they

fur - nish me ___ with tape. ___ But deep in - side ___ my heart ___ I

Chorus

know I ___ can't es - cape. ___ Oh, ___ Ma - ma, can this real -

- ly be ___ the end, ___ to be stuck ___ in - side ___ of Mo - bile with the

Mem - phis blues ___ a - gain? ___ 2. Well,

1.- 8. 9.

Additional Lyrics

2. Well, Shakespeare, he's in the alley
   With his pointed shoes and his bells,
   Speaking to some French girl
   Who says she knows me well.
   And I would send a message
   To find out if she's talked,
   But the post office has been stolen
   And the mailbox is locked.

3. Mona tried to tell me
   To stay away from the train line.
   She said that all the railroad men
   Just drink up your blood like wine.
   An' I said, "Oh, I didn't know that,
   But then again, there's only one I've met,
   An' he just smoked my eyelids
   An' punched my cigarette."

4. Grandpa died last week
   And now he's buried in the rocks.
   But everybody still talks about
   How badly they were shocked.
   But me, I expected it to happen.
   I knew he'd lost control
   When he built a fire on Main Street
   And shot it full of holes.

5. Now, the senator came down here
   Showing everyone his gun,
   Handing out free tickets
   To the wedding of his son.
   An' me, I nearly got busted,
   An' wouldn't it be my luck
   To get caught without a ticket
   And be discovered beneath a truck.

6. Now, the preacher looked so baffled
   When I asked him why he dressed
   With twenty pounds of headlines
   Stapled to his chest.
   But he cursed me when I proved to him,
   Then I whispered, said, "Not even you can hide.
   You see, you're just like me.
   I hope you're satisfied."

7. Now, the rainman gave me two cures,
   Then he said, "Jump right in."
   The one was Texas medicine,
   The other was just railroad gin.
   An' like a fool I mixed them,
   An' it strangled up my mind,
   An' now people just get uglier,
   An' I have no sense of time.

8. When Ruthie says come see her
   In her honky-tonk lagoon,
   Where I can watch her waltz for free
   'Neath her Panamanian moon.
   An' I say, "Aw come on, now,
   You know, you know about my debutante."
   An' she says, "Your debutante just
   Knows what you need,
   But I know what you want."

9. Now the bricks lay on Grand Street,
   Where the neon madmen climb.
   They all fall there so perfectly;
   It all seems so well timed.
   An' here I sit so patiently,
   Waiting to find out what price
   You have to pay to get out of
   Going through all these things twice.

Standard Ukulele

Baritone Ukulele

Guitar

Mandolin

Banjo

Subterranean Homesick Blues
Words and Music by Bob Dylan

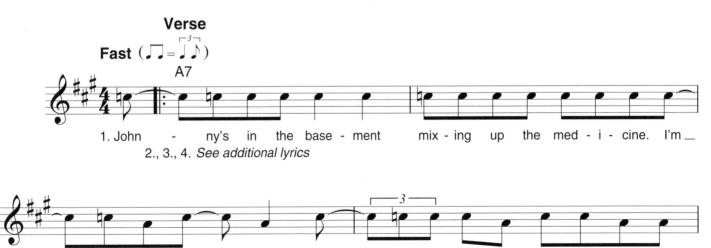

1. John - ny's in the base - ment mix - ing up the med - i - cine. I'm
2., 3., 4. *See additional lyrics*

___ on the pave - ment think - ing a - bout the gov - ern - ment. A

man in a trench coat, badge out, laid ___ off, says he's got a bad cough,

D7

wants to get it paid off. Look out, kid, it's some-thin' you did. ___ God ___

A7

___ knows when, but you're do-in' it a-gain. You bet-ter duck down the al-ley-way,

E7 *3*

look-in' for a new friend. The man in the coon-skin cap ___ in a big pen ___ wants e-

A7 *3*

lev-en dol-lar bills. ___ You on-ly got ___ ten.

1., 2., 3. **4.**

2. Mag -

Additional Lyrics

2. Maggie comes fleet-foot,
   Face full of black soot.
   Talkin' that the heat put
   Plants in the bed, but
   The phone's tapped anyway.
   Maggie says that many say
   They must bust in early May,
   Orders from the D.A.
   Look out, kid,
   Don't matter what you did.
   Walk on your tiptoes,
   Don't try NoDoz.
   Better stay away from those
   That carry around a fire hose.
   Keep a clean nose,
   Watch the plain clothes.
   You don't need a weatherman
   To know which way the wind blows.

3. Ah, get sick, get well,
   Hang around a ink well.
   Ring bell, hard to tell
   If anything is gonna sell.
   Try hard, get barred,
   Get back, write Braille.
   Get jailed, jump bail,
   Join the army, if you fail.
   Look out, kid,
   You're gonna get hit.
   But losers, cheaters,
   Six-time users
   Hangin' 'round the theaters.
   Girl by the whirlpool
   Lookin' for a new fool.
   Don't follow leaders;
   Watch the parkin' meters.

4. Ah, get born, keep warm.
   Short pants, romance, learn to dance.
   Get dressed, get blessed,
   Try to be a success.
   Please her, please him, buy gifts,
   Don't steal, don't lift.
   Twenty years of schoolin'
   And they put you on the day shift.
   Look out, kid,
   They keep it all hid.
   Better jump down a manhole,
   Light yourself a candle.
   Don't wear sandals;
   Try to avoid the scandals.
   Don't wanna be a bum;
   You better chew gum.
   The pump don't work
   'Cause the vandals took the handles.

Standard Ukulele

Baritone Ukulele

Guitar

Mandolin

Banjo

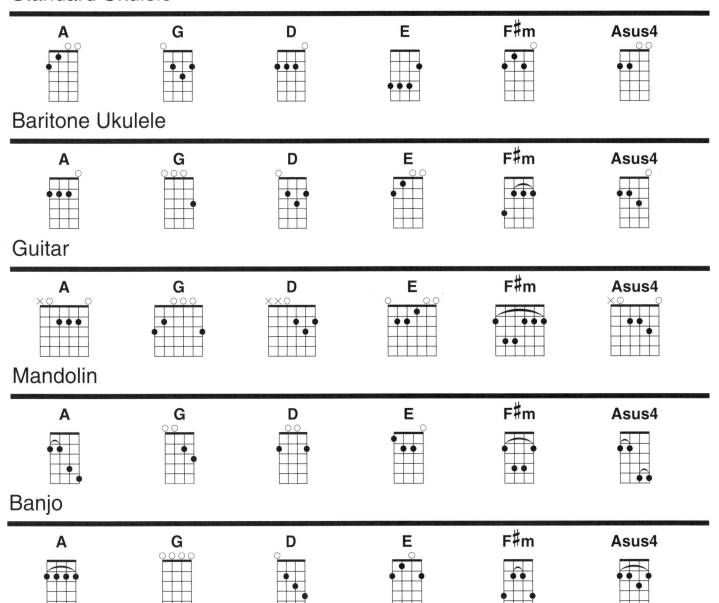

Tangled Up in Blue
Words and Music by Bob Dylan

Verse
Moderately, in 2

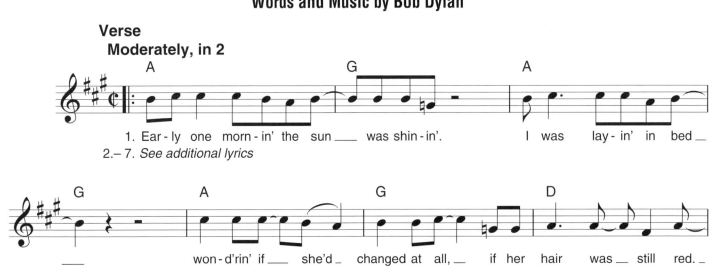

1. Ear-ly one morn-in' the sun ___ was shin-in'. I was lay-in' in bed ___
2.–7. *See additional lyrics*

___ won-d'rin' if ___ she'd ___ changed at all, ___ if her hair was ___ still red. ___

Her folks, they said our lives ___ to-geth-er sure was gon-na be rough. ___
They nev-er did like ___ Ma-ma's home-made dress; ___ Pa-pa's
bank book was ___ n't big e - nough. And I was stand - in' on the
side of the road, ___ rain ___ fall - in' on my shoes, ___
head - ing up for the East ___ Coast. Lord knows, I've paid some dues ___
___ get - tin' through. ___ Tan - gled up in blue. ___

Play 7 times

Additional Lyrics

2. She was married when we first met, soon to be divorced.
   I helped her out of a jam, I guess, but I used a little too much force.
   We drove that car as far as we could, abandoned it out West,
   Split up on a dark, sad night, both agreeing it was best.
   As she turned around to look at me as I was a-walkin' away,
   I heard her say over my shoulder, "We'll meet again someday
   On the avenue."
   Tangled up in blue.

3. I had a job in the Great North Woods, working as a cook for a spell.
   But I never did like it all that much, and one day the axe just fell.
   So I drifted down to New Orleans, where I lucky was to be employed,
   Workin' for a while on a fishin' boat right outside of Delacroix.
   But all the while I was alone, the past was close behind.
   I seen a lot of women, but she never escaped my mind, and I
   Just grew
   Tangled up in blue.

4. She was workin' in a topless place and I stopped in for a beer.
   I just kept lookin' at the side of her face in the spotlight so clear.
   And later on when the crowd thinned out, I's just about to do
   The same.
   She was standin' there in back of my chair, said to me, "Don't
   I know your name?"
   I muttered somethin' underneath my breath, she studied the
   Lines on my face.
   I must admit I felt a little uneasy when she bent down to tie the
   Laces of my shoe.
   Tangled up in blue.

5. She lit a burner on the stove and offered me a pipe.
   "I thought you'd never say hello," she said. "You look like the
   Silent type."
   Then she opened up a book of poems and handed it to me,
   Written by an Italian poet from the fifteenth century.
   And every one of them words rang true and glowed like
   Burnin' coal,
   Pourin' off of every page like it was written in my soul from
   Me to you.
   Tangled up in blue.

6. I lived with them on Montague Street in a basement
   Down the stairs.
   There was music in the cafés at night and revolution in
   The air.
   Then he started into dealing with slaves and something
   Inside of him died.
   She had to sell everything she owned and froze up inside.
   And when, finally, the bottom fell out, I became withdrawn.
   The only thing I knew how to do was to keep on keepin' on
   Like a bird that flew.
   Tangled up in blue.

7. So now I'm goin' back again; I got to get to her somehow.
   All the people we used to know, they're an illusion to me now.
   Some are mathematicians, some are carpenter's wives.
   Don't know how it all got started; I don't know what they're
   Doin' with their lives.
   But me, I'm still on the road, headin' for another joint.
   We always did feel the same; we just saw it from a different
   Point of view.
   Tangled up in blue.

Standard Ukulele

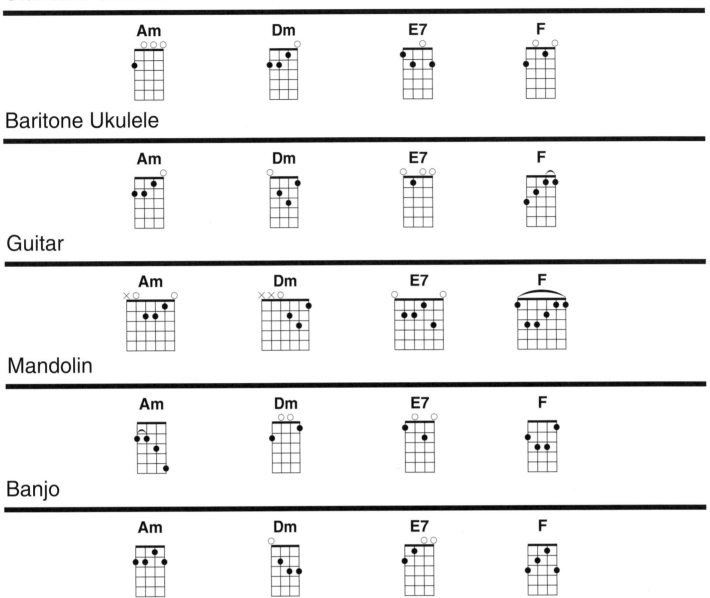

Baritone Ukulele

Guitar

Mandolin

Banjo

Things Have Changed

Words and Music by Bob Dylan

Verse
Moderately

Am

1. A wor-ried man with a wor-ried mind,

Dm

no one in front of me and

Am

noth-ing be-hind. ___ There's a wom-an on my lap ___ and she's drink-ing cham -

2.– 4. *See additional lyrics*

Additional Lyrics

2. This place ain't doing me any good.
   I'm in the wrong town, I should be in Hollywood.
   Just for a second there I thought I saw something move.
   Gonna take dancing lessons, do the jitterbug rag.
   Ain't no shortcuts, gonna dress in drag.
   Only a fool in here would think he's got anything to prove.
   Lot of water under the bridge, lot of other stuff too.
   Don't get up, gentlemen, I'm only passing through.

3. I've been walking forty miles of bad road.
   If the Bible is right, the world will explode.
   I've been trying to get as far away from myself as I can.
   Some things are too hot to touch.
   The human mind can only stand so much.
   You can't win with a losing hand.
   Feel like falling in love with the first woman I meet,
   Putting her in a wheelbarrow and wheeling her down the street.

4. I hurt easy, I just don't show it.
   You can hurt someone and not even know it.
   The next sixty seconds could be like an eternity.
   Gonna get low down, gonna fly high.
   All the truth in the world adds up to one big lie.
   I'm in love with a woman who don't even appeal to me.
   Mr. Jinx and Miss Lucy, they jumped in the lake.
   I'm not that eager to make a mistake.

Standard Ukulele

Baritone Ukulele

Guitar

Mandolin

Banjo

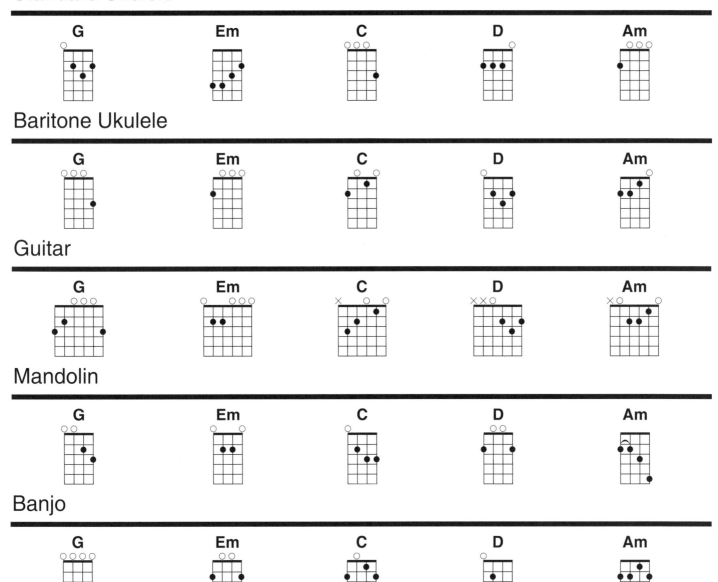

The Times They Are A-Changin'

Words and Music by Bob Dylan

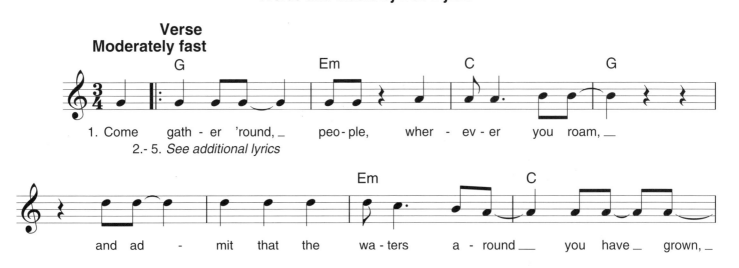

1. Come gath-er 'round, _ peo-ple, wher-ev-er you roam, _
2.- 5. *See additional lyrics*

and ad-mit that the wa-ters a-round __ you have _ grown, _

Additional Lyrics

2. Come writers and critics who prophesize with your pen,
   And keep your eyes wide, the chance won't come again.
   And don't speak too soon for the wheel's still in spin,
   And there's no tellin' who that it's namin'.
   For the loser now will be later to win,
   For the times they are a-changin'.

3. Come senators, congressmen, please heed the call.
   Don't stand in the doorway, don't block up the hall,
   For he that gets hurt will be he who has stalled.
   There's a battle outside ragin'.
   It'll soon shake your windows and rattle your walls,
   For the times they are a-changin'.

4. Come mothers and fathers throughout the land,
   And don't criticize what you can't understand.
   Your sons and your daughters are beyond your command.
   Your old road is rapidly agin'.
   Please get out of the new one if you can't lend your hand,
   For the times they are a-changin'.

5. The line it is drawn, the curse it is cast.
   The slow one now will later be fast,
   As the present now will later be past.
   The order is rapidly fadin',
   And the first one now will later be last,
   For the times they are a-changin'.

Standard Ukulele

Baritone Ukulele

Guitar

Mandolin

Banjo

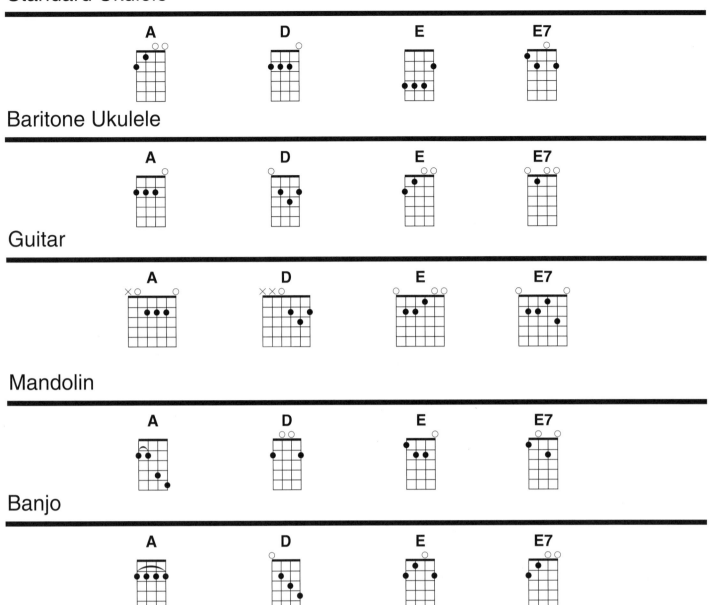

Tomorrow Is a Long Time

Words and Music by Bob Dylan

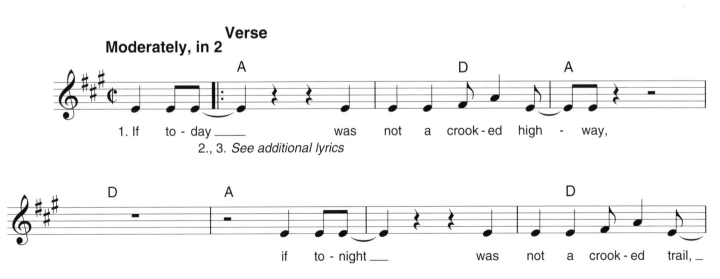

1. If to-day _____ was not a crook-ed high-way,
2., 3. *See additional lyrics*

if to-night _____ was not a crook-ed trail, _____

Chorus

if to-mor-row was-n't such a long __

__ time, then lone-some __ would mean noth-ing to you __ at all.

Yes, and on-ly if my own true love was wait-

-ing, if I could hear her heart __ a-soft-ly pound-ing,

yes, and on-ly if she __ was ly-ing by __ me,

I'd lie __ in my bed __ once __ a-gain. __

2. I can't see __
3. There's beau -

Additional Lyrics

2. I can't see my reflection in the water.
   I can't speak the sounds to show no pain.
   I can't hear the echo of my footsteps
   Or remember the sounds of my own name.

3. There's beauty in that silver, singin' river.
   There's beauty in that rainbow in the sky.
   But none of these and nothing else can touch the beauty
   That I remember in my true love's eyes.

Standard Ukulele

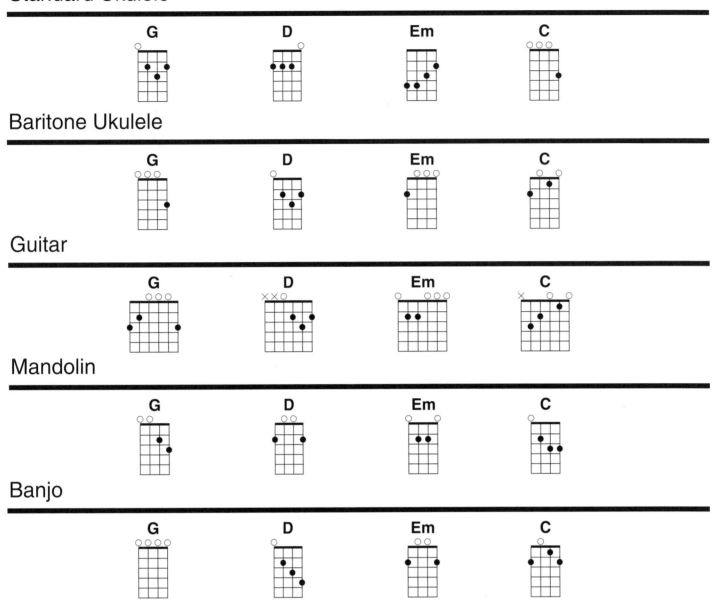

Baritone Ukulele

Guitar

Mandolin

Banjo

Wagon Wheel

Words and Music by Bob Dylan and Ketch Secor

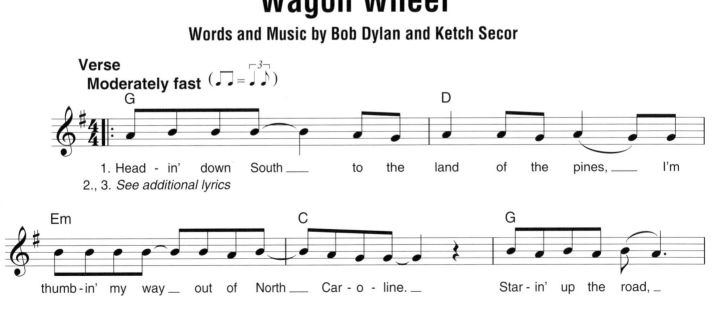

1. Head - in' down South ___ to the land of the pines, ___ I'm
2., 3. *See additional lyrics*

thumb - in' my way ___ out of North ___ Car - o - line. ___ Star - in' up the road, ___

Additional Lyrics

2. Runnin' from the cold up in New England,
I was born to be a fiddler in an old-time string band.
My baby plays the guitar; I pick a banjo now.
Oh, North Country winters keep a-gettin' me down.
Lost my money playin' poker, so I had to up and leave.
But I ain't turnin' back to livin' that old life no more.

3. Walkin' through the South out of Roanoke,
I caught a trucker out of Philly, had a nice long toke.
But he's a-headed west from the Cumberland Gap
To Johnson City, Tennessee.
And I gotta get a move on before the sun.
I hear my baby callin' my name and I know that
She's the only one.
And if I die in Raleigh, at least I will die free.

Standard Ukulele

Baritone Ukulele

Guitar

Mandolin

Banjo

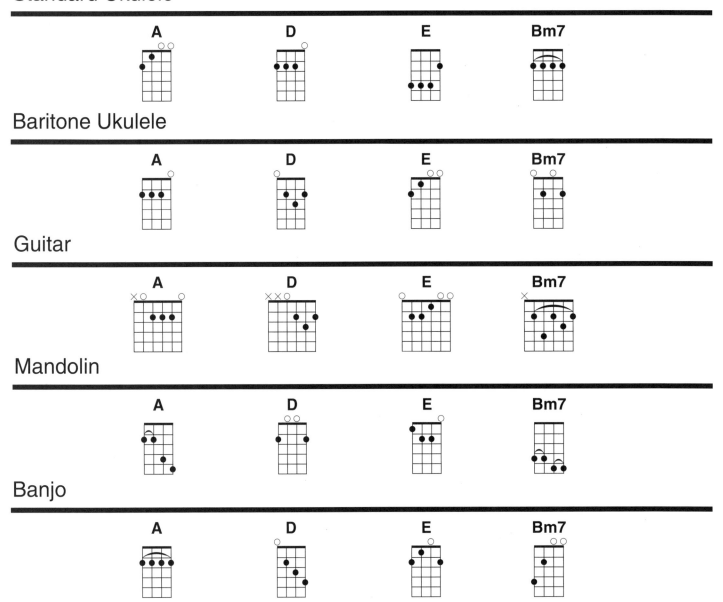

When I Paint My Masterpiece

Words and Music by Bob Dylan

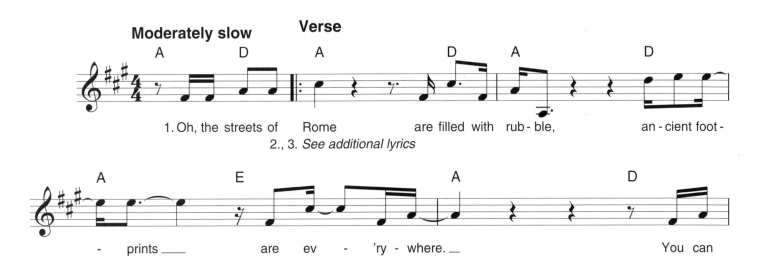

Moderately slow

Verse

1. Oh, the streets of Rome are filled with rub - ble, an - cient foot -

2., 3. *See additional lyrics*

- prints ___ are ev - 'ry - where. ___ You can

al - most think _____ that you're see - in' dou - ble on a

cold, dark night _ on the Span - ish Stairs. _

Got to hur - ry on back _ to my ho - tel room, where I've

got me a date with Bot - ti - cel - li's niece. Yup, she

prom - ised _____ that she'd be right there with me when I

paint _____ my mas - ter - piece. _

2. Oh, the _____
3. I left

Additional Lyrics

2. Oh, the hours that I've spent inside the Coliseum,
   Dodging lions and wastin' time.
   Oh, those mighty kings of the jungle, I could hardly stand to see 'em.
   Yes, it sure has been a long, hard climb.
   Train wheels runnin' through the back of my memory
   As the daylight hours do retreat.
   Someday, everything is gonna be smooth like a rhapsody,
   When I paint my masterpiece.

3. I left Rome and landed in Brussels
   With a picture of a tall oak tree by my side.
   Clergymen in uniform and young girls pullin' muscles;
   Everyone was there but nobody tried to hide.
   Newspapermen eating candy
   Had to be held down by big police.
   Someday, everything is gonna be different,
   When I paint my masterpiece.

Standard Ukulele

Baritone Ukulele

Guitar

Mandolin

Banjo

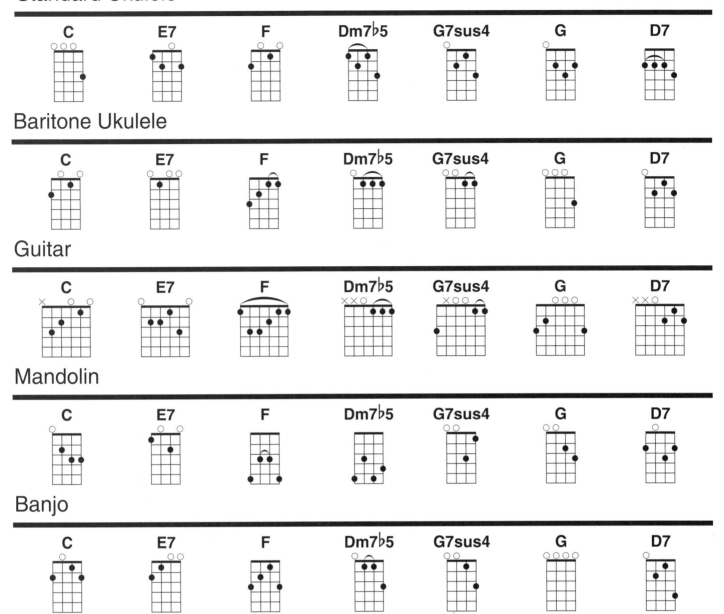

When the Deal Goes Down
Words and Music by Bob Dylan

1. In the still of the night, in the world's _ an-cient light, _ where
2., 3., 4. *See additional lyrics*

wis-dom grows up in strife, my be-wil-dered brain _

Additional Lyrics

2. We eat and we drink, we feel and we think;
Far down the street we stray.
I laugh and I cry and I'm haunted by
Things I never meant nor wished to say.
The midnight rain follows the train.
We all wear the same thorny crown.
Soul to soul, our shadows roll,
And I'll be with you when the deal goes down.

3. Now, the moon gives light and it shines by night;
I scarcely feel the glow.
We learn to live and then we forgive.
O'er the road we're bound to go.
More frailer than the flowers, these precious hours
That keep us so tightly bound.
You come to my eyes like a vision from the skies.
And I'll be with you when the deal goes down.

4. Well, I picked up a rose and it poked through my clothes.
I followed the winding stream.
I heard a deafening noise, I felt transient joys;
I know they're not what they seem.
In this earthly domain, full of disappointment and pain,
You'll never see me frown.
I owe my heart to you, and that's sayin' it true,
And I'll be with you when the deal goes down.

Standard Ukulele

Baritone Ukulele

Guitar

Mandolin

Banjo

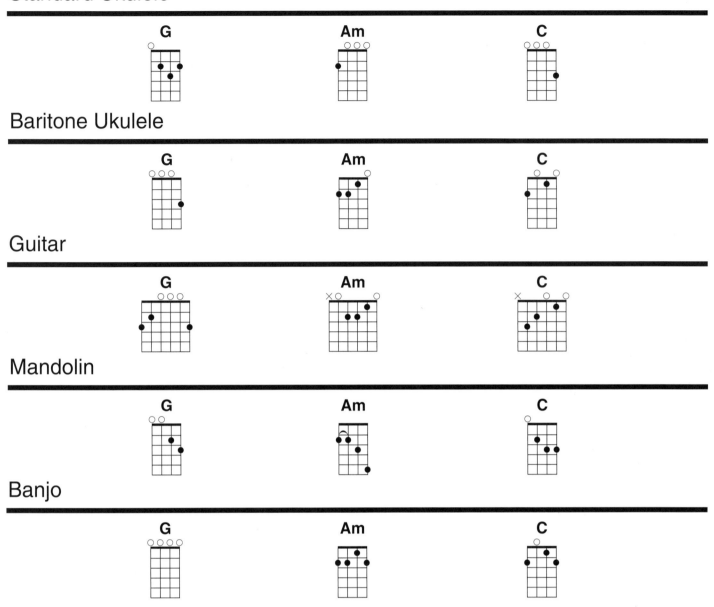

You Ain't Goin' Nowhere
Words and Music by Bob Dylan

Verse
Moderately fast

1. Clouds so swift and rain ____ fall-in' in. ____ Gon - na see a mo-vie called
2., 3. *See additional lyrics*

Gun - ga Din. ____ Pack up your mon - ey, pull up your tent, Mc - Guinn. ____

You ain't a - go - in' no - where. ___

Chorus

Oo - ee, ___

ride me high. ___ To - mor-row's the day ___ that my bride's ___ a - gon - na come. ___

Oo - ee, ___ are we gon - na fly ___ down in - to the eas - y chair? _

1., 2.

3.

Additional Lyrics

2. Genghis Khan and his brother Don
   Couldn't keep on keepin' on.
   We'll climb that bridge after it's gone,
   After we're way past it.

3. Buy me some rings and a gun that sings,
   A flute that toots and a bee that stings,
   A sky that cries and a bird that flies,
   A fish that walks and a dog that talks.

Standard Ukulele

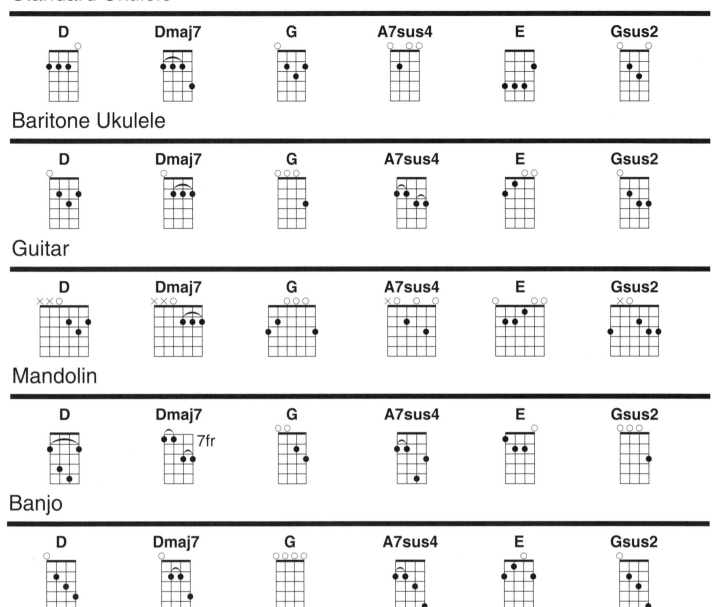

Baritone Ukulele

Guitar

Mandolin

Banjo

You're Gonna Make Me Lonesome
When You Go
Words and Music by Bob Dylan

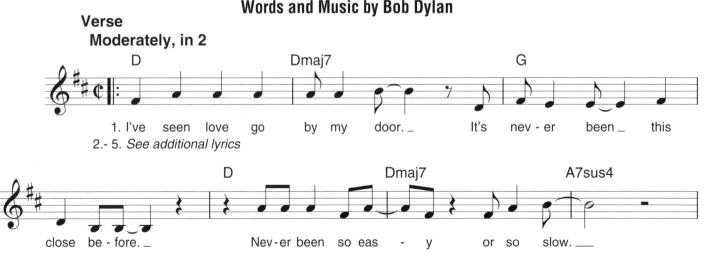

Verse
Moderately, in 2

1. I've seen love go by my door. _ It's nev-er been _ this

2.- 5. *See additional lyrics*

close be-fore. _ Nev-er been so eas - y or so slow. __

Additional Lyrics

2. Dragon clouds so high above.
   I've only known careless love;
   It always has hit me from below.
   But this time 'round it's more correct,
   Right on target, so direct.
   You're gonna make me lonesome when you go.

3. Purple clover, Queen Anne lace,
   Crimson hair across your face,
   You could make me cry, if you don't know.
   Can't remember what I was thinkin' of.
   You might be spoilin' me too much, love.
   You're gonna make me lonesome when you go.

4. Situations have ended sad,
   Relationships have all been bad.
   Mine've been like Verlaine's and Rimbaud.
   But there's no way I can compare
   All them scenes to this affair.
   You're gonna make me lonesome when you go

Bridge 2:
You're gonna make me wonder what I'm doin',
Stayin' far behind without you.
You're gonna make me wonder what I'm sayin'.
You're gonna make me give myself a good talkin' to.

5. I'll look for you in old Honolula,
   San Francisco or Ashtabula.
   You're gonna have to leave me now, I know.
   But I'll see you in the sky above,
   In the tall grass, in the ones I love.
   You're gonna make me lonesome when you go.

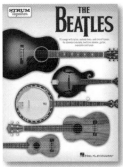

FIRST 50

*Books in the First 50 series contain easy to intermediate arrangements for must-know songs.
Each arrangement is simple and streamlined, yet still captures the essence of the tune.*

First 50 Baroque Pieces
You Should Play on Guitar
Includes selections by Johann Sebastian Bach, Robert de Visée, Ernst Gottlieb Baron, Santiago de Murcia, Antonio Vivaldi, Sylvius Leopold Weiss, and more.
00322567..$14.99

First 50 Bluegrass Solos
You Should Play on Guitar
I Am a Man of Constant Sorrow • Long Journey Home • Molly and Tenbrooks • Old Joe Clark • Rocky Top • Salty Dog Blues • and more.
00298574..$16.99

First 50 Blues Songs
You Should Play on Guitar
All Your Love (I Miss Loving) • Bad to the Bone • Born Under a Bad Sign • Dust My Broom • Hoodoo Man Blues • Little Red Rooster • Love Struck Baby • Pride and Joy • Smoking Gun • Still Got the Blues • The Thrill Is Gone • You Shook Me • and more.
00235790..$17.99

First 50 Blues Turnarounds
You Should Play on Guitar
You'll learn cool turnarounds in the styles of these jazz legends: John Lee Hooker, Robert Johnson, Joe Pass, Jimmy Rogers, Hubert Sumlin, Stevie Ray Vaughan, T-Bone Walker, Muddy Waters, and more.
00277469..$14.99

First 50 Chords
You Should Play on Guitar
American Pie • Back in Black • Brown Eyed Girl • Landslide • Let It Be • Riptide • Summer of '69 • Take Me Home, Country Roads • Won't Get Fooled Again • You've Got a Friend • and more.
00300255 Guitar...................................$12.99

First 50 Classical Pieces
You Should Play on Guitar
Includes compositions by J.S. Bach, Augustin Barrios, Matteo Carcassi, Domenico Scarlatti, Fernando Sor, Francisco Tárrega, Robert de Visée, Antonio Vivaldi and many more.
00155414 ....$16.99

First 50 Folk Songs
You Should Play on Guitar
Amazing Grace • Down by the Riverside • Home on the Range • I've Been Working on the Railroad • Kumbaya • Man of Constant Sorrow • Oh! Susanna • This Little Light of Mine • When the Saints Go Marching In • The Yellow Rose of Texas • and more.
00235868 ....$16.99

First 50 Guitar Duets
You Should Play
Chopsticks • Clocks • Eleanor Rigby • Game of Thrones Theme • Hallelujah • Linus and Lucy (from *A Charlie Brown Christmas*) • Memory (from *Cats*) • Over the Rainbow (from *The Wizard of Oz*) • Star Wars (Main Theme) • What a Wonderful World • You Raise Me Up • and more.
00319706..$14.99

First 50 Jazz Standards
You Should Play on Guitar
All the Things You Are • Body and Soul • Don't Get Around Much Anymore • Fly Me to the Moon (In Other Words) • The Girl from Ipanema (Garota De Ipanema) • I Got Rhythm • Laura • Misty • Night and Day • Satin Summertime • When I Fall in Love • and more.
00198594 Solo Guitar $16.99

First 50 Kids' Songs
You Should Play on Guitar
Do-Re-Mi • Hakuna Matata • Let It Go • My Favorite Things • Puff the Magic Dragon • Take Me Out to the Ball Game • Won't You Be My Neighbor? (It's a Beautiful Day in the Neighborhood) • and more.
00300500 ....$15.99

First 50 Licks
You Should Play on Guitar
Licks presented include the styles of legendary guitarists like Eric Clapton, Buddy Guy, Jimi Hendrix, B.B. King, Randy Rhoads, Carlos Santana, Stevie Ray Vaughan and many more.
00278875 Book/Online Audio.........................$14.99

First 50 Riffs
You Should Play on Guitar
All Right Now • Back in Black • Barracuda • Carry on Wayward Son • Crazy Train • La Grange • Layla • Seven Nation Army • Smoke on the Water • Sunday Bloody Sunday • Sunshine of Your Love • Sweet Home Alabama • Working Man • and more.
00277366..$14.99

First 50 Rock Songs You Should
Play on Electric Guitar
All Along the Watchtower • Beat It • Brown Eyed Girl • Cocaine • Detroit Rock City • Hallelujah • (I Can't Get No) Satisfaction • Oh, Pretty Woman • Pride and Joy • Seven Nation Army • Should I Stay or Should I Go • Smells like Teen Spirit • Smoke on the Water • When I Come Around • You Really Got Me • and more.
00131159 ....$15.99

First 50 Songs by the Beatles You
Should Play on Guitar
All You Need Is Love • Blackbird • Come Together • Eleanor Rigby • Hey Jude • I Want to Hold Your Hand • Let It Be • Ob-La-Di, Ob-La-Da • She Loves You • Twist and Shout • Yellow Submarine • Yesterday • and more.
00295323..$19.99

First 50 Songs
You Should Fingerpick on Guitar
Annie's Song • Blackbird • The Boxer • Classical Gas • Dust in the Wind • Fire and Rain • Greensleeves • Road Trippin' • Shape of My Heart • Tears in Heaven • Time in a Bottle • Vincent (Starry Starry Night) • and more.
00149269 ....$16.99

First 50 Songs You Should
Play on 12-String Guitar
California Dreamin' • Closer to the Heart • Free Fallin' • Give a Little Bit • Hotel California • Leaving on a Jet Plane • Life by the Drop • Over the Hills and Far Away • Solsbury Hill • Space Oddity • Wish You Were Here • You Wear It Well • and more.
00287559..$15.99

First 50 Songs You Should Play on
Acoustic Guitar
Against the Wind • Boulevard of Broken Dreams • Champagne Supernova • Every Rose Has Its Thorn • Fast Car • Free Fallin' • Layla • Let Her Go • Mean • One • Ring of Fire • Signs • Stairway to Heaven • Trouble • Wagon Wheel • Yellow • Yesterday • and more.
00131209 ....$16.99

First 50 Songs
You Should Play on Bass
Blister in the Sun • I Got You (I Feel Good) • Livin' on a Prayer • Low Rider • Money • Monkey Wrench • My Generation • Roxanne • Should I Stay or Should I Go • Uptown Funk • What's Going On • With or Without You • Yellow • and more.
00149189 ....$16.99

First 50 Songs
You Should Play on Solo Guitar
Africa • All of Me • Blue Skies • California Dreamin' • Change the World • Crazy • Dream a Little Dream of Me • Every Breath You Take • Hallelujah • Wonderful Tonight • Yesterday • You Raise Me Up • Your Song • and more.
00288843 ....$17.99

First 50 Songs
You Should Strum on Guitar
American Pie • Blowin' in the Wind • Daughter • Hey, Soul Sister • Home • I Will Wait • Losing My Religion • Mrs. Robinson • No Woman No Cry • Peaceful Easy Feeling • Rocky Mountain High • Sweet Caroline • Teardrops on My Guitar • Wonderful Tonight • and more.
00148996 Guitar..................................$16.99

HAL•LEONARD®
www.halleonard.com

0922
014

Get Better at Guitar

...with these Great Guitar Instruction Books from Hal Leonard!

101 GUITAR TIPS
INCLUDES TAB

STUFF ALL THE PROS KNOW AND USE
by Adam St. James
This book contains invaluable guidance on everything from scales and music theory to truss rod adjustments, proper recording studio set-ups, and much more.

00695737 Book/Online Audio $17.99

AMAZING PHRASING
INCLUDES TAB

by Tom Kolb
This book/audio pack explores all the main components necessary for crafting well-balanced rhythmic and melodic phrases. It also explains how these phrases are put together to form cohesive solos. The companion audio contains 89 demo tracks, most with full-band backing.

00695583 Book/Online Audio $22.99

ARPEGGIOS FOR THE MODERN GUITARIST
INCLUDES TAB

by Tom Kolb
Using this no-nonsense book with online audio, guitarists will learn to apply and execute all types of arpeggio forms using a variety of techniques, including alternate picking, sweep picking, tapping, string skipping, and legato.

00695862 Book/Online Audio $22.99

BLUES YOU CAN USE

by John Ganapes
This comprehensive source for learning blues guitar is designed to develop both your lead and rhythm playing. Includes: 21 complete solos • blues chords, progressions and riffs • turnarounds • movable scales and soloing techniques • string bending • utilizing the entire fingerboard • and more.

00142420 Book/Online Media $22.99

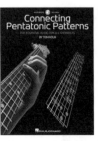

CONNECTING PENTATONIC PATTERNS
INCLUDES TAB

by Tom Kolb
If you've been finding yourself trapped in the pentatonic box, this book is for you! This hands-on book with online audio offers examples for guitar players of all levels, from beginner to advanced. Study this book faithfully, and soon you'll be soloing all over the neck with the greatest of ease.

00696445 Book/Online Audio $24.99

FRETBOARD MASTERY
INCLUDES TAB

by Troy Stetina
Untangle the mysterious regions of the guitar fretboard and unlock your potential. This book familiarizes you with all the shapes you need to know by applying them in real musical examples, thereby reinforcing and reaffirming your newfound knowledge.

00695331 Book/Online Audio $22.99

GUITAR AEROBICS
INCLUDES TAB

by Troy Nelson
Here is a daily dose of guitar "vitamins" to keep your chops fine tuned! Musical styles include rock, blues, jazz, metal, country, and funk. Techniques taught include alternate picking, arpeggios, sweep picking, string skipping, legato, string bending, and rhythm guitar.

00695946 Book/Online Audio $24.99

GUITAR CLUES
INCLUDES TAB

OPERATION PENTATONIC
by Greg Koch
Whether you're new to improvising or have been doing it for a while, this book/audio pack will provide loads of delicious licks and tricks that you can use right away, from volume swells and chicken pickin' to intervallic and chordal ideas.

00695827 Book/Online Audio $19.99

PAT METHENY – GUITAR ETUDES
INCLUDES TAB

Over the years, in many master classes and workshops around the world, Pat has demonstrated the kind of daily workout he puts himself through. This book includes a collection of 14 guitar etudes he created to help you limber up, improve picking technique and build finger independence.

00696587 .... $17.99

PICTURE CHORD ENCYCLOPEDIA

This comprehensive guitar chord resource for all playing styles and levels features five voicings of 44 chord qualities for all twelve keys – 2,640 chords in all! For each, there is a clearly illustrated chord frame, as well as *an actual photo* of the chord being played!.

00695224 .... $22.99

RHYTHM GUITAR 365
INCLUDES TAB

by Troy Nelson
This book provides 365 exercises – one for every day of the year! – to keep your rhythm chops fine tuned. Topics covered include: chord theory; the fundamentals of rhythm; fingerpicking; strum patterns; diatonic and non-diatonic progressions; triads; major and minor keys; and more.

00103627 Book/Online Audio $27.99

SCALE CHORD RELATIONSHIPS
INCLUDES TAB

by Michael Mueller & Jeff Schroedl
This book/audio pack explains how to: recognize keys • analyze chord progressions • use the modes • play over nondiatonic harmony • use harmonic and melodic minor scales • use symmetrical scales • incorporate exotic scales • and much more!

00695563 Book/Online Audio $17.99

SPEED MECHANICS FOR LEAD GUITAR
INCLUDES TAB

by Troy Stetina
Take your playing to the stratosphere with this advanced lead book which will help you develop speed and precision in today's explosive playing styles. Learn the fastest ways to achieve speed and control, secrets to make your practice time really count, and how to open your ears and make your musical ideas more solid and tangible.

00699323 Book/Online Audio $22.99

TOTAL ROCK GUITAR
INCLUDES TAB

by Troy Stetina
This comprehensive source for learning rock guitar is designed to develop both lead and rhythm playing. It covers: getting a tone that rocks • open chords, power chords and barre chords • riffs, scales and licks • string bending, strumming, and harmonics • and more.

00695246 Book/Online Audio $22.99

Guitar World Presents STEVE VAI'S GUITAR WORKOUT
INCLUDES TAB

In this book, Steve Vai reveals his path to virtuoso enlightenment with two challenging guitar workouts – one 10-hour and one 30-hour – which include scale and chord exercises, ear training, sight-reading, music theory, and much more.

00119643 .... $16.99